joy

OF CARD MAKING

collector's edition

**PaperCrafts** MAGAZINE®  Joy of Card Making: Collector's Edition

## Editorial

Editor-in-Chief  Stacy Croninger
Managing Editor  Kimberly Carroll
Creative Editor  Cath Edvalson
Editor  Brandy Jesperson
Associate Creative Editor  Megan Hoeppner
Associate Editor  P. Kelly Smith
Copy Editor  Melanie King
Editorial Assistant  Brenda Peterson
Senior Web Editor  Ana Cabrera
Associate Web Editor  Christy Shepherd

## Design

Art Director  Stace Hasegawa
Designer  Celeste Rockwood-Jones
Photography  Skylar Nielson

## Advertising & Events

Advertising Sales U.S. & International  Donna Summers, 815/389-3289
Online and Interactive Sales  Jackie Baillie, 801/816-8331
Directory Sales Manager  Kristi Larsen, 801/816-8362
VP/Director of Events  Paula Kraemer
Events Coordinators  Emily Haskell, Vicki Manning, Brooke Mathewson
Assistant Events Coordinators  Annette Hardy, Marie Rappleye, Micaela Zoeller

## Operations

Production Director  Tom Stuber
Administrative Assistant  Alicia Pearman

## Offices

Editorial  *Paper Crafts* magazine, 14850 Pony Express Rd., Bluffdale, UT 84065-4801
Phone  801/816-8300
Fax  801/816-8301
E-mail  *editor@PaperCraftsMag.com*
Web site  *www.PaperCraftsMag.com*

Published by Leisure Arts, Inc., 5701 Ranch Drive, Little Rock, Arkansas 72223-9633. 501-868-8800. www.leisurearts.com

Library of Congress Control Number: 2008921953
ISBN-13: 978-1-60140-842-6
ISBN-10: 1-60140-842-0

## Leisure Arts Staff

Managing Editor  Susan White Sullivan
Special Projects Director  Susan Frantz Wiles
Director of Designer Relations  Debra Nettles
Senior Prepress Director  Mark Hawkins
Publishing Systems Administrator  Becky Riddle
Publishing Systems Assistants  Clint Hanson, John Rose, Keiji Yumoto, and Carrie East

Vice President and Chief Operating Officer  Tom Siebenmorgen
Director of Corporate Planning and Development  Laticia Mull Dittrich
Vice President, Sales and Marketing  Pam Stebbins
Director of Sales and Services  Margaret Reinold
Vice President, Operations  Jim Dittrich
Comptroller, Operations  Rob Thieme
Retail Customer Service Manager  Stan Raynor
Print Production Manager  Fred F. Pruss

## CK Media, LLC

Chief Executive Officer  David O'Neil
Group Publisher/Quilting  Tina Battock
VP/Editorial Director  Lin Sorenson
Chief Marketing Officer  Andrew Johnson
VP/Consumer Marketing Director  Susan DuBois
Circulation Director  Catherine Flynn
VP/Online Director  Chad Phelps

PUBLICATION—*Joy of Card Making: Collector's Edition* is a special issue of *Paper Crafts*™ magazine. *Paper Crafts*™ (ISSN 0148-9127) is published 8 times per year in February, March, April/May, June/July, Aug/Sept, October, November, and Dec/Jan by CK Media, LLC., 14850 Pony Express Rd., Bluffdale, Utah 84065. Phone: 212/448-4573. Fax: 212/448-4790. Periodicals postage paid at Bluffdale, UT, and additional mailing offices.

RATES—Single-copy sale for *Paper Crafts*™ in the U.S. and its possessions, $4.99; Canadian, $5.99. Subscription rate for U.S. and its possessions, one year $19.97; Canadian subscriptions add $12 per year (includes GST tax, Canadian GST R126520923); Foreign subscriptions add $20 per year; total amount payable in U.S. funds only. Some back issues are available for $6.99 each, payable in advance. Call 801/984-2070. Advertising rates furnished on request. Call 309/679-5302.

REPRINT PERMISSION—For information on obtaining reprints and excerpts, please contact Wright's Reprints at 877/652-5295. (Customers outside the U.S. and Canada should call 281/419-5725.)

SUBMISSIONS—Send sketches, photos, and proposals (not finished projects) to *Paper Crafts* magazine, Attn.: Submissions, 14850 Pony Express Rd., Bluffdale, UT 84065-4818, or e-mail to *specials@PaperCraftsMag.com*. *Paper Crafts* is not responsible for lost or mutilated manuscripts. Payment for projects is made upon publication, current rates prevailing.

# For the collector in us all!

I love getting magazines throughout the year, whether they are for paper crafting, cooking, or some other fun hobby. The anticipation of the next issue is almost more than I can stand. But then comes the dilemma—what to keep. In a perfect world, I'd keep every issue so I could refer back to them when I need inspiration or a new idea. But like you, I have limited storage space.

I think that's why I love collector's editions. They are compact, filled with favorites, and a great reference. Such is the case with *Joy of Card Making: Collector's Edition*. In one great book, you'll find recipes for card designs and examples that will inspire you. The card recipes are some of our favorites. At the back of the book, you'll find an index of recipes that is sure to be a great resource. And, everything is bound together for easy storage and quick reference.

But remember, while collecting is fun, creating is much more rewarding. So, grab your supplies and let the creativity begin.

Stacy C

# Tried and True

While home visiting my parents for Thanksgiving last year, my mom and I carefully planned our Thanksgiving dinner, making sure to include the family's favorites. As we discussed the recipes for salads, homemade rolls, and desserts, I realized that we always went back to her tried and true recipes from my childhood. As I leafed through her recipes, a wave of memories came over me as I remembered sitting at the kitchen counter watching the big mixer go round and round, whipping up yummy chocolate chip cookies or chocolate sheet cake. As a child (and even now), I couldn't wait to lick the bowl and spoon after the mixing was complete.

The recipes found in her box are filled with years of traditions and memories. They have all been gathered in one place to refer to time after time, never to let us down as we come together for her famous cooking.

Like my mother's recipes, this collection of card recipes remains the same. Each is considered tried and true as paper crafters from all over the world have used these again and again to create handmade cards to share with those they love. We've gathered these recipes together in one place; one that is filled to the brim with delicious ideas that will bring you back again and again.

Wendy

# contents

127

101

210

As classic as your mom's pot roast, these card designs are based on the classic size of 4¼" x 5½". You'll find an abundance of recipes in this chapter to tantalize your creative taste buds and give you the zest to create handmade expressions of love.

Bountiful in size and design, the recipes in this chapter are two delicious sizes: 4" x 9" and 3⅜" x 6". These recipes are so fun and versatile, you'll want to create a second helping of cards!

Whip up your own perfectly square cards for every occasion based on the plentiful recipes in this chapter.

Cook up cards in no time with these simple recipes. The small 3" x 3½" size is perfect to attach to gifts but still brimming with flavor.

Sample the unique card designs in this chapter. With fabulous folds, appetizing pull-outs, and fancy shapes, these recipes are just right for any sweet occasion!

52

120

# CHAPTER 1

# Card Classics

As classic as your mom's pot roast, these card designs

are based on the standard size of 4¼" x 5½". You'll

find an abundance of recipes in this chapter to tantalize

your creative taste buds and give you the zest to create

handmade expressions of love.

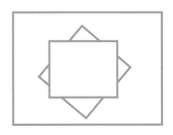

## Hi You

Designer: Angelia Wigginton

### SUPPLIES

**Cardstock:** (Teal) *Bazzill Basics Paper* **Patterned paper:** (School's Out from Road Trip collection) *Scrapworks*; (Blueberry from Lollipop Shoppe collection) *BasicGrey* **Accents:** (fabric stencil letters) *Scrapworks*; (white stone letters) *EK Success* **Fibers:** (white thread)

### INSTRUCTIONS

❶ Make card from cardstock. ❷ Cut School's Out paper to fit card front. Trim edges and zigzag-stitch. ❸ Cut square of Blueberry paper; stitch edges and adhere to card. ❹ Trim fabric stencil letters and attach to card. ❺ Adhere white stone letters to spell "You".

### SECRET INGREDIENT

*When stitching accents, stitch each individual piece before attaching it to the card front so the stitching can't be seen from the inside of the card.*

## Congrats Tag
Designer: Wendy Johnson

SUPPLIES
**Textured cardstock:** (Lily White, Pebble) *Bazzill Basics Paper* **Paper:** (red from Second Avenue Congrats collection) *My Mind's Eye* **Patterned paper:** (brown circles from Second Avenue Congrats collection) *My Mind's Eye* **Color medium:** (gray chalk) *Craf-T Products* **Accents:** (metal alphabet) *Making Memories*; (diploma) *My Mind's Eye* **Fibers:** (red ribbon) *Making Memories*; (black, gray, white striped grosgrain ribbon) *Michaels*
MAKES ONE 4" x 5½" TAG

### APPETIZING IDEAS
*Chalk the edges of the Lily White cardstock with gray chalk to blend it into the Pebble cardstock.*

*Trim the paper bow from the diploma and add ribbon to give it a dimensional, realistic effect.*

## Monogram Diamonds
Designer: Sara Horton

SUPPLIES
**Patterned paper:** (Midnight Diamonds, Midnight Paisley from A Day to Remember collection) *Bo-Bunny Press*; (Tattered Red) *Scissor Sisters* **Dye ink:** (Coal Black) *Clearsnap* **Stickers:** (Elegant alphabet) *Bo-Bunny Press*

## Celebrating the Graduate
Designer: Alisa Bangerter

SUPPLIES
**Cardstock:** (Silver) *Paper Garden*; (black) **Paint:** (Black) *Delta* **Accents:** (black tassel) *Impress Rubber Stamps*; (aluminum sheet) *Ten Seconds Studio*; (aluminum metal mesh) *Making Memories* **Tools:** (various decorative wheels, point, brass brush, small ball and cup, small fined dots, thin foam mat, acrylic mat) *Ten Seconds Studio* **Other:** (vinyl spackling) *Ace Hardware*

### APPETIZING IDEAS
*Place foam mat on acrylic mat. Place aluminum sheet face down on foam mat. Run various decorative wheels around edge of aluminum sheet.*

*There are many different decorative wheels from Ten Seconds Studio that can be used on aluminum and cardstock to give added dimension and texture.*

*Rub paint over the edges of the cardstock, metal mesh, and embellishment to accent the design.*

sentiment

## Belted Birthday

Designer: Wendy Johnson

### SUPPLIES

**Cardstock:** (white, red, light blue) **Patterned paper:** (Brite Red White Blue) Perky Plaids, *Keeping Memories Alive* **Acrylic paint:** (Aquamarine) Tropic, Scrapbook Colors, *Making Memories* **Accent:** (Large Square 2 Ribbon Charm) *Making Memories* **Fibers:** (happy birthday ribbon) *Impress Rubber Stamps* **Adhesive:** (foam tape) Scotch, *3M*; dots **Tools:** (Pom Pom, circle punches) *EK Success*; paintbrush, scissors

### INSTRUCTIONS

❶ Paint ribbon charm and set aside to dry. ❷ Make card from white cardstock. ❸ Cut Brite Red White Blue paper to fit ¾ of card front; adhere. ❹ Punch three flowers from red cardstock and three circles from light blue cardstock; adhere circles to flowers. ❺ Adhere flowers to card with foam tape. ❻ Thread ribbon through ribbon charm and adhere to card.

## Nautical Dad

Designer: Marla Bird

SUPPLIES

**Textured cardstock:** (Wonderful White, Cameo Cream) *Pebbles in my Pocket;* (Lava, Arctic) *Bazzill Basics Paper* **Accent:** (Nickel Ring) Gypsy Hardware, *7gypsies* **Fasteners:** (large silver eyelets) *Memory Lane Paper Co.* **Fibers:** (Sisal Twine) Eco Africa, *Provo Craft* **Rub-ons:** (Stamped White alphabet) *Autumn Leaves* **Adhesive:** (machine) *Xyron;* (craft glue) Aleene's Original Tacky Glue, *Duncan* **Tools:** (1" circle punch) *Family Treasures;* eyelet-setting tools, scissors

## Antique Love

Designer: Sande Krieger

SUPPLIES

**Cardstock:** (tan) **Patterned paper:** (Dictionary) Life's Journey, *K&Company* **Dye ink:** (Van Dyke Brown) Nick Bantock, *Ranger Industries* **Paper accent:** (Love flash card) Word Art Cards, *The Weathered Door* **Accent:** (hinge with brads) *The Weathered Door* **Fibers:** (brown ribbon) *The Weathered Door* Adhesive **Tools:** scissors

**TIP A LA SANDE**

*Cut the Love flash card into strips and ink the edges before adhering it to the card for added dimension and interest.*

## Kick Back

Designer: Kathleen Paneitz

SUPPLIES

**Cardstock:** (white) **Patterned paper:** (W1) Get Happy, *Sweetwater* **Specialty paper:** (Burgundy canvas) Textured Accents, *K&Company* **Accents:** (red staples, oval label holder) *Making Memories* **Sticker:** (Vacation) Like It Is, *Making Memories* **Rub-on:** (kick back from Vacation) Simply Stated Mini, *Making Memories* **Fibers:** (blue twine) *All My Memories* **Adhesive Tools:** scissors, sandpaper, stapler

# Hanukkah Stripes

Designer: Nichole Heady

SUPPLIES

**Cardstock:** (Brilliant Blue, Ultrasmooth White) *Stampin' Up!* **Rubber stamps:** (Star of David from Year-Round Fun set, Simple Stripes background) *Stampin' Up!* **Dye ink:** (Brilliant Blue) *Stampin' Up!* **Solvent ink:** (Ultramarine) StāzOn, *Tsukineko* **Fibers:** (blue) Brights, Fancy Fibers, *Stampin' Up!* **Font:** (Schindler Small Caps) *Microsoft* **Shrink plastic:** *Lucky Squirrel* **Tools:** (1⅜" circle punch) *EK Success*; (hole punch) *Fiskars*; scissors, computer and printer, oven, baking sheet

# Cheerful Get Well

Designer: Wendy Sue Anderson

SUPPLIES

**Cardstock:** (Cotton Candy Solid) Eye Candy, Collection III, *KI Memories* **Patterned paper:** (Runway, Blossom) Eye Candy, Collection III, *KI Memories* **Dye ink:** (Sand) Memories, *Stewart Superior Corp.* **Sticker:** (Sentiments 2) Wonderful Words, Dèjá Views, *C-Thru Ruler Co.* **Fastener:** (flower eyelet) Classy Accents, *Dolphin Enterprises* **Fibers:** (pink stitched ribbon) *Making Memories* **Tools:** eyelet-setting tools, scissors

# Hanging Tree

Designer: Wendy Johnson

### SUPPLIES

**Textured cardstock:** (Dark Black) *Bazzill Basics Paper* **Patterned paper:** (Deep Red Heritage Stripe Dark) Heritage Collection, *Making Memories* **Paper:** (white) **Accent:** (metal tree) Charmed Plaques, *Making Memories* **Fasteners:** (red brads) *Impress Rubber Stamps* **Fibers:** (black and white gingham ribbon) *Offray* **Font:** (CurlzMT) WordPerfect, *Corel* **Adhesive** **Tools:** scissors, computer and printer

### INSTRUCTIONS

❶ Make card from Dark Black cardstock.
❷ Cut Deep Red Heritage Stripe Dark patterned paper slightly smaller than card front. ❸ Print sentiment on white paper; trim and mat with Dark Black. ❹ Attach brads to three corners of sentiment.
❺ Cut small length of ribbon and adhere ends to back of tree accent. Attach to remaining corner of sentiment with brad.
❻ Adhere sentiment and tree accent to Deep Red Heritage Stripe Dark rectangle; adhere rectangle to card.

## Framed Daisy

Designer: Kathleen Paneitz

**SUPPLIES**

**Cardstock:** (white) **Patterned paper:** (Runway) Beautiful, Collection III, *KI Memories* **Paper accent:** (pink daisy) Blossoms, *Making Memories* **Accents:** (Checkered frame) Charmed Frames, (silver jump ring) *Making Memories*; (metal tag) *Creative Impressions*; (thank you) Ice Candy, *KI Memories* **Fibers:** (brown stitched ribbon) *May Arts* **Adhesive:** metal, glue stick **Tools:** scissors

## Flamingo Birthday

Designer: Ann Powell

**SUPPLIES**

**Patterned paper:** (Pink Tiny Stripes) Celebration Series, Cutie Pie Flip Flop Papers, *Keeping Memories Alive* **Transparency sheet:** *Hammermill* **Rubber stamp:** (flamingo from Tickled Pink set) *Stampin' Up!* **Solvent ink:** (Jet Black) StāzOn, *Tsukineko* **Color media:** (pink, blue, orange, yellow markers) Fabrico, *Tsukineko* **Dimensional glaze:** Crystal Effects, *Stampin' Up!* **Accents:** (pink slide holder) *Magic Scraps*; (pink wire) *Making Memories*; (silver jump ring) **Fonts:** (Proud Papa, Dream, Fairy Princess) www.twopeasinabucket.com **Shrink plastic:** *Stampin' Up!* **Adhesive:** foam tape, dots **Tools:** scissors, computer and printer, oven, baking sheet **Other:** Flamingo charm made by Marissa Jones

**TIP A LA ANN**

*Marker ink applied to shrink plastic will darken as the plastic shrinks. To create shading and lighter colors, blot excess ink with a paper towel before it dries.*

## Anniversary Script

Designer: Dee Gallimore-Perry

**SUPPLIES**

**Cardstock:** (Black) *Bazzill Basics Paper* **Patterned paper:** (Sommes) *7gypsies* **Paper accents:** (metal-rimmed vellum tag) Tagged, (happy anniversary tag) Calendar Events, Cardstock Tags, *Making Memories*; (heart square) Black & White Blox, Collection I, *KI Memories* **Fibers:** (black and white ribbon), (I Love You ribbon) Ribbon Words, *Making Memories* **Adhesive:** (liquid) KI Gloo, *KI Memories* **Tools:** sewing machine, scissors **Other:** white thread

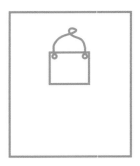

## Flower Plaque

Designer: Wendy Johnson

### SUPPLIES

**Textured cardstock:** (Flamingo, Aloe Vera, Wisteria) *Bazzill Basics Paper* **Cardstock:** (White) *Bazzill Basics Paper* **Rubber stamps:** (daisy from Whimsical Flowers set) *Hero Arts*; (thank you) *Savvy Stamps* **Dye ink:** (Black) *The Angel Company* **Color media:** (Orchid Opulence marker) Stampin' Write, *Stampin' Up!*; (watercolor pencils) Prismacolor, *Sanford* **Accent:** (silver wire) *Darice* **Fasteners:** (mini purple eyelets) *Making Memories*; (white brad) **Tools:** (blender pen) *Dove Brushes*; (air art tool) Inkworx, *Stampin' Up!*; eyelet-setting tools, scissors

### INSTRUCTIONS

❶ Make card from Flamingo cardstock. ❷ Stamp daisy on White cardstock; trim. Color with watercolor pencils; blend. ❸ Splatter daisy rectangle with Orchid Opulence marker and air art tool. ❹ Mat daisy rectangle with Aloe Vera and Wisteria cardstock, tearing bottom edge of each mat. ❺ Cut 5" length of wire; twist at center to form loop. ❻ Attach eyelets to top two corners of daisy rectangle. Thread wire ends through eyelets and secure in back. ❼ Attach wire loop to card with brad. Adhere daisy rectangle to card. ❽ Stamp thank you.

## Chic Baby

Designer: Marla Bird

### SUPPLIES

**Patterned paper:** (Floral) Garden Scrap Pad, *Provo Craft* **Color medium:** (brown chalk) **Accents:** (silver jump rings), (rocking horse charm from Nursery set) Changlz, *Provo Craft*; (slide mount) *Creative Imaginations* **Adhesive:** (craft glue) Aleene's Original Tacky Glue, *Duncan* **Tools:** chalk applicator, scissors **Other:** Ivy sprig

## Framed Tree

Designer: Wendy Sue Anderson

### SUPPLIES

**Cardstock:** (brick red) **Patterned paper:** (Wildgrass Canvas) Embellishment Paper, *Making Memories*; (Stripe-Pinecone) *Daisy D's* **Acrylic paint:** (Evergreen, Cranberry) Harvest, Scrapbook Colors, *Making Memories* **Accents:** (Happy Holidays frame) Charmed Frames, (tree charm) Charmed, *Making Memories* **Fastener:** (silver brad) *Creative Impressions* **Fibers:** (green gingham ribbon) *Offray* **Tools:** paintbrush, scissors

### TIP A LA WENDY SUE

*Use baby wipes to wipe excess paint off metal frame and charm. Wipe excess paint off immediately, as it dries quickly.*

## Sweet of You

Designer: Nichole Heady

SUPPLIES

*All supplies from Stampin' Up! unless otherwise noted.*

**Cardstock:** (Chocolate Chip, Blush Blossom, Ultrasmooth White) **Patterned paper:** (Pink Cherry Blossom) Over the Moon Press, *EK Success* **Rubber stamps:** (Sweet of You set) **Dye ink:** (Chocolate Chip) **Fastener:** (silver brad) **Adhesive:** no source **Tools:** (¹⁄₁₆" hole punch) *Fiskars*; (scissors) no source

### HOW TO make purse

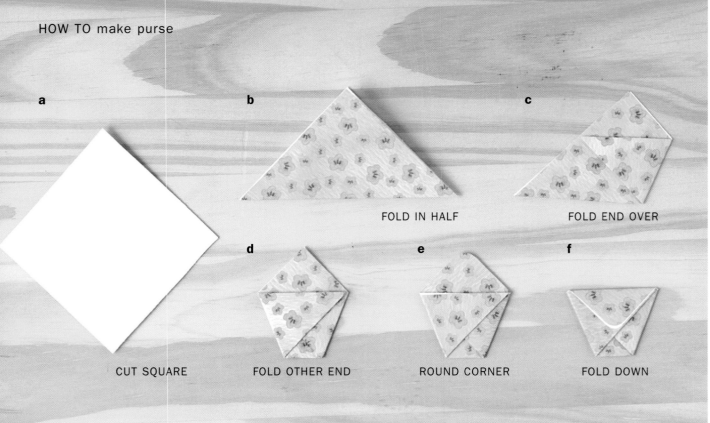

a

b — FOLD IN HALF

c — FOLD END OVER

CUT SQUARE

d — FOLD OTHER END

e — ROUND CORNER

f — FOLD DOWN

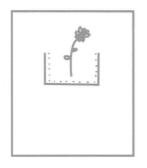

## Treats for the Sweet
Designer: Wendy Johnson

### SUPPLIES

**Cardstock:** (Bubblegum, Blue Jay) *Bazzill Basics Paper* **Textured cardstock:** (Raven) *Bazzill Basics Paper* **Patterned paper:** (Pink Check) *Daisy D's* **Accent:** (lollipop) Gingerbread Visions, *NSI Innovations* **Stickers:** (clear alphabet stickers) Brad Alphabets, *Making Memories* **Fasteners:** (blue brads) *Making Memories* **Fonts:** (Proud Papa, Bleached Blonde, Blueberry Pie) *www.two-peasinabucket.com* **Fibers:** (pink ribbon) *Offray*; (blue rickrack) **Tools:** scissors, sewing machine, computer and printer **Other:** white thread, white copy paper

### INSTRUCTIONS

❶ Make card from Bubblegum cardstock; cut Raven cardstock slightly smaller than card front and adhere. Straight-stitch around edge of Raven rectangle. ❷ Cut rectangle of Pink Check paper; straight-stitch around edges and adhere rickrack to top. ❸ Place brads at bottom right of patterned paper rectangle; spell "SWEET" with brad stickers. ❹ Print "you're so sweet!" in each font on white paper; cut out and mat with Blue Jay or Bubblegum cardstock. ❺ Tie ribbon bow around lollipop. Adhere lollipop and sentiments to center of card; Pink Check rectangle over top. *Note: Pink Check rectangle creates pocket.*

## Thinking of You

Designer: Sande Krieger

SUPPLIES

**Patterned paper:** (Faux Pink Mulberry, Light Brown Speckle) *Keeping Memories Alive* **Specialty paper:** (Cream floral embossed) Paper Passport, *Provo Craft* **Rubber stamps:** (Typewriter Alphabet) *Hero Arts* **Pigment ink:** (Brown) ColorBox, *Clearsnap* **Paper accent:** (Vintage Butterfly) *NRN Designs* **Accent:** (rhinestone) **Tools:** scissors, sewing machine **Other:** black thread, sandpaper

## Dad

Designer: Kathleen Paneitz

SUPPLIES

**Cardstock:** (brown) **Textured cardstock:** (cream) **Patterned paper:** (Yellow Stripe) Life's Journey, *K&Company* **Accent:** (brown tag pocket) The Attic Collection, *EK Success* **Rub-ons:** (White Stamped alphabet) *Autumn Leaves* **Stickers:** (Fresh Fish from Old Rooster Café) *Karen Foster Design* **Fastener:** (washer eyelet) *Creative Impressions* **Fibers:** (black gingham ribbon) *Offray* **Tools:** scissors, eyelet-setting tools **Other:** sandpaper

### ADD SOME FLAVOR

*Add a little bit of fishing flair by stringing your ribbon along with a fishhook or two on some fishing line at the top of the tag. Make sure to bend the ends with a pair of pliers to get rid of the sharp points.*

# Friendship Flower

Designer: Michelle Tardie

SUPPLIES

**Textured cardstock:** (Dark Tangerine) Chatterbox Collection, *Bazzill Basics Paper* **Patterned paper:** (Sun-Kissed Yellow Plaid) *Patchwork Paper Design* **Paper accent:** (vellum envelope) *EK Success* **Stickers:** (epoxy flower from Garden Bubbles) David Walker, *Creative Imaginations*; (Friendship quote) Tiny Tale, *My Mind's Eye*; (vellum "friends") Friendship Thoughts, *O'Scrap!* **Fibers:** (orange gingham ribbon) *Offray* **Tools:** scissors

# Three Candles

Designer: Dee Gallimore-Perry

SUPPLIES

**Cardstock:** (yellow) **Patterned paper:** (Raspberry Bangles) Lava Lamp, Collection III, *KI Memories* **Dye ink:** (Basic Black) *Stampin' Up!* **Paper accents:** (candles) Frame-Ups, *My Mind's Eye* **Accents:** (plastic slide holder sleeve) *C-Line Products*; (black wire) *Artistic Wire*; (make a wish woven label) Birthday Threads, *Me & My Big Ideas* **Tools:** scissors, sewing machine **Other:** white thread, sandpaper

## APPETIZING IDEA

*Cut the flames off of the candles and reattach them with the black wire.*

## SECRET INGREDIENT

*Love stitching but hate the mess that shows up on the inside of your card? Stitch embellishments to your patterned paper, and then adhere the patterned paper to the card front as the last step.*

sentiment

# Gift from the Heart

Designer: Wendy Johnson

**SUPPLIES**

**Cardstock:** (Chili) *Bazzill Basics Paper*
**Textured cardstock:** (Olive, Watermelon) *Bazzill Basics Paper* **Patterned paper:** (Green & Red Stripe) Tulip Collection, *K&Company* **Paper accent:** (kraft bag) *DMD, Inc.* **Fibers:** (white string) **Font:** (David Walker) *www.twopeasinabucket.com* **Accents:** (staples) **Adhesive:** (foam tape) *3M* **Tools:** (heart punch) *EK Success*; scissors, stapler, mini hole punch, computer and printer **Other:** tissue paper

**BAG ACCENT**

❶ Punch heart from Watermelon cardstock. ❷ Adhere heart to Chili cardstock with foam tape; cut into tag shape. Mat with Olive cardstock; punch hole at top. ❸ Attach string to tag; knot. ❹ Cut rectangle of tissue paper; crumple and place inside kraft bag with gift. ❺ Fold down bag top; staple tag string to top of bag.

**CARD**

❶ Make card from Olive cardstock. ❷ Cut Green & Red Stripe paper slightly smaller than card front; adhere. ❸ Print "for you" on Watermelon cardstock; cut out and mat with Olive. ❹ Adhere "for you" with foam tape to bottom right corner. ❺ Adhere bag accent to center of card front.

## Bunny Treats

Designer: Kathleen Paneitz

SUPPLIES
**Cardstock:** (Easter) Companion Series, *American Crafts*; (white) **Accent:** (Easter Basket) Jolee's By You, *EK Success* **Rub-ons:** (white alphabet) Itty Bitty, *Doodlebug Design*; (Pastel Alphabet) *Li'l Davis Designs* **Tools:** scissors

## Anniversary Gift

Designer: Lori Allred

SUPPLIES
**Patterned paper:** (Red Fine-Weave Linen) *Bo-Bunny Press* **Acrylic paint:** (Spotlight) Cityscape, Scrapbook Colors, *Making Memories* **Paper accents:** (always, together from Love) Cardstock Tags, *Making Memories*; (kraft bag) **Rub-on:** (Happy Anniversary) Paper Bliss, *Westrim Crafts* **Fibers:** (red gingham ribbon) **Tools:** scissors, sponge paintbrush **Other:** gift card

### SPICE IT UP
*If you don't want to include a gift card, replace the brown bag with a picture of the couple. Then tie the word tags and ribbon around the bottom of the picture.*

*Replace the word tags with ring, heart, or wedding charms.*

## Bits of Stardust

Designer: Lori Allred

SUPPLIES
**Cardstock:** (Buttercup Pinstripe, Buttercup Polka Dot) *Making Memories*; (cream) **Font:** (Fontdiner Loungy) www.fontdiner.com **Accents:** (mini organza bag) Bag Its, *The Craft Pedlars*; (star confetti) *Jones Tones* **Tools:** scissors, computer and printer

### TIP A LA LORI
*Take a card from flat to 3-D by using foam tape or dimensional adhesive dots. Dimensional adhesive is a great way to pop up the sentiment or another accent and make it the focal point of your card.*

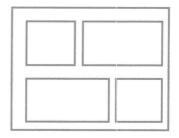

## Fun

Designer: Wendy Johnson

### SUPPLIES

**Cardstock:** (Celery) Savory, *SEI*; (white, blue)
**Acrylic paint:** (Blueberry, Daiquiri from
Sherbet set; Meadow from In Bloom set)
Scrapbook Colors, *Making Memories* **Paper
accents:** (Poolside Mod Blox & Circle Tags)
Collection III, *KI Memories* **Accent:** (silver
concho) *Scrapworks* **Fibers:** (green ribbons)
*Making Memories* **Adhesive:** (foam tape) *3M*;
glue stick **Tools:** scissors, paintbrushes

### INSTRUCTIONS

❶ Make card from Celery cardstock.
❷ Cut white cardstock slightly smaller than
card front. ❸ Apply Blueberry, Daiquiri, and
Meadow paint to white rectangle. *Note:
Lightly apply paint to brush and move in
circular motion.* ❹ Adhere loops of ribbon
to back of paper accents; adhere paper
accents to blue cardstock with foam tape.
Cut out and adhere to painted cardstock
piece. ❺ Adhere painted cardstock piece
to front of card.

## Plumeria Sympathy

Designer: Nichole Heady

SUPPLIES
**Cardstock:** (Confetti Cream) *Stampin' Up!*
**Patterned paper:** (Script) *Life's Journey,*
*K&Company;* (Plumeria) *Creative Imaginations*
**Dye ink:** (Creamy Caramel) *Stampin' Up!*
**Accents:** (brown seed beads) *Crafts, Etc.*
**Sticker:** (remember from Capture the Moment set)
*Twill Expressions, All My Memories* Dimensional
glaze: Crystal Effects, *Stampin' Up!* **Tools:** scissors, wire brush, craft knife

### APPETIZING IDEA

*Use a craft knife to cut around
the magnolia petals and square.*

## Baby Blue

Designer: Dee Gallimore-Perry

SUPPLIES
*All supplies from KI Memories unless
otherwise noted.*

**Cardstock:** (Sea Breeze) Expecting, Collection IV
**Patterned paper:** (Expecting Pop, Expecting
Wisdom from Expecting set) Collection IV **Paper
accents:** (Expecting Mod Blox & Tags, Expecting
Frames & Labels) Collection IV **Rub-on:** (heart
outline) White Graphic Icons, Collection IV **Fibers:**
(Celery ribbon) *Making Memories* **Adhesive:**
(dots) *Glue Dots International* **Tools:** (sewing
machine, scissors) no source **Other:** (white
thread) no source

### TIP A LA DEE

*Add a little pizzazz to a flat design
by using dimensional adhesive, stitching,
or by adding ribbon.*

## My Friend

Designer: Ann Powell

SUPPLIES
**Patterned paper:** (Pink Speckle) Hippie Chick,
*SEI* **Stickers:** (Black Bubbletters & Middles)
Collection III, *KI Memories;* (Large Black Just
My Type, Small Black Just My Type alphabets)
*Doodlebug Design;* (Typewriter Alphabet) *Limited
Edition Rubberstamps* **Fibers:** (black gingham
ribbon) *Offray* **Tools:** (circle punch) *Marvy
Uchida;* scissors

### SPICE IT UP

*Use this same design for mom, dad, grandparents,
or siblings, and use up those extra alphabet
stickers you have lying around!*

## All Boy

Designer: Wendy Johnson

SUPPLIES

**Cardstock:** (white, black) **Patterned paper:** (Blue Check) *Daisy D's* **Accents:** (bottle caps) *Li'l Davis Designs* **Rub-ons:** (bottle cap alphabet) *Li'l Davis Designs* **Fibers:** (black gingham ribbon) *Making Memories* **Tools:** scissors, craft knife, ruler

INSTRUCTIONS

❶ Make card from white cardstock; cut 1" off bottom of card front. ❷ Cut rectangle of black cardstock; adhere to card front with edge slightly over bottom of card front. ❸ Cut rectangle of blue gingham paper to fit card front; adhere. ❹ Cut slit in fold at one end of card; thread ribbon through slit and knot on card front. ❺ Apply rub-ons to bottle caps to spell "BOY." ❻ Adhere bottle caps to bottom edge of card front. *Note: Allow caps to hang over edge.*

## No Place Like Home

Designer: Sande Krieger

SUPPLIES

**Textured cardstock:** (Nutmeg) *Bazzill Basics Paper*
**Patterned paper:** (Stucco Motif, Ochre) *Motifica
Collection, BasicGrey* **Accents:** (pewter buttons)
*Jo-Ann Stores* **Rub-ons:** (There's No Place Like
Home from Family set) *Love Notes, Chatterbox*
**Tools:** scissors, hole punch

### TIP A LA SANDE
*Cutting shanks off of buttons can be tricky.
To save time, punch a hole in the paper where you
want to place the button; insert the shank through
that hole when adhering and you won't have to
worry about the extra dimension.*

## Floral Promise

Designer: Nichole Heady

SUPPLIES

**Cardstock:** (Baroque Burgundy) *Stampin' Up!*
**Patterned paper:** (Fleur Rouge) *Anna Griffin;*
(Script) *7gypsies* **Dye ink:** (Tea Dye) *Tim Holtz
Distress Ink, Ranger Industries* **Dimensional
glaze:** Crystal Effects, *Stampin' Up!* **Accents:**
(Promise/Forever/Always zipper pulls) *All My
Memories* **Fibers:** (red ribbons) *Making Memories*
**Tools:** scissors

### SPICE IT UP
*Change the look of your card by simply cutting
and adhering the script patterned paper
so the text is running the opposite direction. Now
your card is based on a top-fold design.*

*Make this card for any occasion by leaving
off the charms and embellishing the edge
with ribbons. Punch three or more holes
along the edge, thread the ribbons through
the holes, knot, and trim the excess.*

## It's Your Day

Designer: Michelle Tardie

SUPPLIES

**Textured cardstock:** (Dark Olive, Dark Black)
*Bazzill Basics Paper* **Patterned paper:** (Antique
Dot Cream) *Daisy D's* **Pigment ink:** (Black)
*ColorBox, Clearsnap* **Accent:** (It's Your Day)
Woven Labels, *Making Memories* **Fasteners:**
(black photo turn) *Making Memories;* (black brad)
*Karen Foster Design* **Fibers:** (brown gingham
ribbon) *Impress Rubber Stamps* **Tools:** scissors

### SPICE IT UP
*Change to another hip color for a whole new look.
Try hot or light pink for the girly girl, baby blue or
turquoise for retro, or red for a rustic country feel.*

sentiment

## Flowered Thanks

Designer: Wendy Johnson

SUPPLIES

Cardstock: (white) Patterned paper: (Light Blue Plaid, Pink Dots) Paper Pizazz, *Hot Off The Press* Accents: (thanks from Thank You 2) Jellies, (pink leather flowers) *Making Memories* Fasteners: (white brads) *Impress Rubber Stamps* Tools: scissors

INSTRUCTIONS

① Make card from white cardstock. ② Cut Pink Dots paper to fit card front; adhere. ③ Cut Light Blue Plaid paper to fit card front; tear bottom edge and adhere. ④ Attach leather flowers to top right corner with white brads. ⑤ Apply thanks accent to bottom center of card front.

### SPICE IT UP

*Try substituting Making Memories Blossoms for the leather flowers to achieve a delicate, all-paper look.*

## What's Up?

**Designer: Kathleen Paneitz**

SUPPLIES

**Textured cardstock:** (Sunbeam) *Bazzill Basics Paper* **Patterned paper:** (Lava Lamp Rhinestone Reverse) Lava Lamp, Collection III, *KI Memories* **Pigment ink:** (Pumpkin) *Stampabilities* **Accents:** (pink mailbox alphabet) *Making Memories* **Rubons:** (Bubble Gum Large alphabet) *Doodlebug Design* **Fastener:** (yellow washer eyelet) *Creative Impressions* **Fibers:** (yellow polka-dot organza ribbon) *May Arts* **Tools:** scissors, eyelet-setting tools

**SECRET INGREDIENT**
*Save time by using a pre-made tag instead of making your own out of white cardstock and an eyelet.*

## Love & Sympathy

**Designer: Sande Krieger**

SUPPLIES

**Patterned paper:** (Reading Poppies, Holiday Stripe) Reading Room, *Chatterbox* **Accent:** (wood button) *Jo-Ann Stores* **Rub-ons:** (Vacation, Wedding, White Heidi) Simply Stated Alphabets, *Making Memories* **Fibers:** (green twill ribbon) *Scenic Route Paper Co.* **Tools:** scissors, sewing machine **Other:** white thread

## Weathered Thanks

**Designer: Michelle Tardie**

SUPPLIES

**Textured cardstock:** (Dark Burgundy) *Bazzill Basics Paper* **Patterned papers:** (Cabin Plaid) Cabin Collection, *Chatterbox* **Vellum:** (Burgundy Daisy) Cabin Collection, *Chatterbox* **Pigment ink:** (Black) ColorBox, *Clearsnap* **Paper accents:** (frames) Cabin Collection, *Chatterbox*; (rustic red wood frame) This & That, *My Mind's Eye* **Color medium:** (metallic rub-on finish) *Craf-T Products* **Fasteners:** (black brads) *Karen Foster Design* **Fibers:** (jute) **Stickers:** (Bubble Type Black alphabet) Little Trinkets and Treasures, *Li'l Davis Designs* **Tools:** scissors

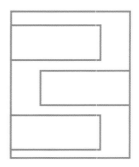

## Many Thanks

Designer: Wendy Johnson

### SUPPLIES

**Cardstock:** (lime green) **Textured cardstock:** (Dark Black) *Bazzill Basics Paper* **Patterned paper:** (blue/green plaid, blue speck, solid blue) *Keeping Memories Alive* **Rub-ons:** (gracias, merci, thank you from Thank You) *Simply Stated Mini, Making Memories* **Fibers:** (white ribbon) *Making Memories* **Font:** (Falling Leaves) *www.twopeasinabucket.com* **Adhesive:** (foam tape) *3M*; glue stick **Tools:** (flower, circle punches) *EK Success*; (scissors, sewing machine) **Other:** white thread

### INSTRUCTIONS

❶ Make card from Dark Black cardstock.
❷ Cut strips of lime green cardstock, and blue/green plaid paper, blue speck, and solid blue paper. Straight-stitch strips to front of card. ❸ Apply gracias rub-on to blue/green plaid, merci rub-on to solid blue, and thank you rub-on to blue speck; cut into tags and mat with Dark Black.
❹ Punch flowers and circles from papers and cardstocks. ❺ Adhere circles to flowers, and flowers to ends of tags; adhere tags to card front with foam tape.

## Congrats Grad

Designer: Ann Powell

SUPPLIES
**Textured cardstock:** (Dark Black) *Bazzill Basics Paper* **Patterned paper:** (diamonds, stripe, black words) *Close To My Heart* **Rubber stamps:** (Aspire, Success, Achieve, Experience from Express It) Magnetic Date Stamp, *Making Memories* **Dye ink:** (Black Soot) Tim Holtz Distress Ink, *Ranger Industries* **Accents:** (black photo turn) *7gypsies;* (black staples) *Making Memories* **Fastener:** (black brad) *Making Memories* **Fibers:** (lace) *Rusty Pickle;* (red/black ribbons) *May Arts* **Font:** (Metallic Avocado) *www.freetypewriterfonts.com* **Adhesive:** spray, glue stick **Tools:** scissors, stapler, sewing machine, computer and printer **Other:** vellum, red thread

### APPETIZING IDEA
*Print the sentiment on vellum and allow it plenty of time to dry before tearing the edges. When adhering vellum use either a spray or vellum adhesive or adhere only an edge of the vellum and cover it with another accent.*

## Be You

Designer: Michelle Tardie

SUPPLIES
**Cardstock:** (Grey Blue Plaid, Orange Dot, Burgundy Plaid, Army Green Plaid) *O'Scrap!* **Rub-ons:** (laugh, dream, be you from Words set) Collage Rub-ons, *Li'l Davis Designs* **Stickers:** (flower, leaves, polka dots from Outdoors set) Simple Squares, *O'Scrap!* **Tools:** scissors

## Baby Doll

Designer: Marla Bird

SUPPLIES
**Textured cardstock:** (textured white) **Patterned paper:** (Rosey Posie) Powder Room, *Chatterbox* **Rubber stamps:** (Pixie Lowercase Alphabet) *Hero Arts* **Pigment ink:** (Velvet) ColorBox, *Clearsnap* **Accents:** (pink safety pins) *Making Memories;* (staples) **Tools:** scissors, stapler, sewing machine **Other:** white thread

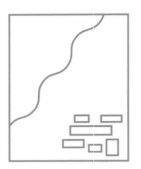

## Butterfly Thinking of You

Designer: Wendy Johnson

### SUPPLIES

**Cardstock:** (light purple, white) **Textured cardstock:** (Heather) *Bazzill Basics Paper* **Patterned paper:** (Purple Plaid) *All My Memories* **Accent:** (butterfly) Tokens, *Doodlebug Design* **Fibers:** (purple gingham ribbon) *May Arts* **Font:** (Spacey Jane) *www.twopeasinabucket.com* **Tools:** scissors, computer and printer **Other:** white copy paper

### INSTRUCTIONS

❶ Make card from white cardstock.
❷ Cut Purple Plaid paper and Heather cardstock to fit card front; adhere Purple Plaid to card. ❸ Cut rectangle of white cardstock to fit width of card; tear off one corner and adhere to top of card. ❹ Tear corner off Heather rectangle and adhere to card. ❺ Print "thinking of you" on white paper. Cut out and mat with light purple cardstock. Cut two small rectangles of Purple Plaid; adhere all to bottom corner of card. ❻ String fiber through butterfly accent; knot. Adhere to card.

## Fall in Love

Designer: Wendy Sue Anderson

SUPPLIES
**Cardstock:** (Ice Blue Polka Dot) *Making Memories*
**Accent:** (jump rings) *Making Memories* **Stickers:**
(Wedding words) Wordfetti, *Making Memories*
**Fibers:** (white organza ribbon) *Offray* **Tools:** scissors

### APPETIZING IDEA
*Instead of tearing off the top corner
and adhering the rest of the paper to the card
front, adhere the top corner. This way
you can use your scraps for a second card!*

## Special Baby

Designer: Nichole Heady

SUPPLIES
**Cardstock:** (Oyster) *Bazzill Basics Paper*
**Patterned paper:** (Camouflage Barcode,
Camouflage Graph) Camouflage, Collection II, *KI
Memories* **Stickers:** (Special from Descriptions)
Wordz, Art Warehouse, *Creative Imaginations*;
(Dark Green Alpha Rounds) Time Savers, *All My
Memories*; (adorable, beautiful from Childhood
set) Wordfetti, *Making Memories*; (vintage
postage stamp) **Tools:** scissors

## The World Is Your Canvas

Designer: Marla Bird

SUPPLIES
**Textured cardstock:** (Walnut, Forget-Me-Not,
Parakeet, Apricot, Sunbeam, Lava, Blue) *Bazzill
Basics Paper* **Specialty paper:** (Ink Jet Canvas)
*Office Max* **Accents:** (alphabet/number charms)
*Making Memories*; (paintbrush) **Rub-on:** (The
World is Your Canvas from Art set) Graffiti Small
Impressions, Art Warehouse, *Creative
Imaginations* **Tools:** scissors

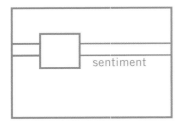

sentiment

## Life's an Adventure

Designer: Alisa Bangerter

### SUPPLIES

**Cardstock:** (white) **Patterned paper:** (Daiquiri Polka Dot, Mango Random Stripe from Sherbet collection) *Making Memories* **Acrylic stamps:** (Sans Small Caps alphabet set) *Close To My Heart* **Dye ink:** (Only Orange) *Stampin' Up!* **Paper accents:** (orange flowers) *Prima* **Accents:** (white snaps) *Making Memories*; (fabric sentiment) *Me & My Big Ideas* **Fibers:** (white twill ribbon) *Wrights*; (white thread) **Adhesive:** (pop-up dots) *Plaid*

### INSTRUCTIONS

❶ Make card from cardstock. ❷ Trim patterned papers to fit card front; stitch to card. ❸ Knot twill ribbon; adhere over paper seam and around card front. ❹ Attach snaps to flowers. ❺ Mat fabric label with cardstock; adhere two flowers to label. ❻ Adhere label to card with pop-up dots. ❼ Stamp "Enjoy your trip" on cardstock; trim, stitch around edges. ❽ Adhere flower and sentiment to card.

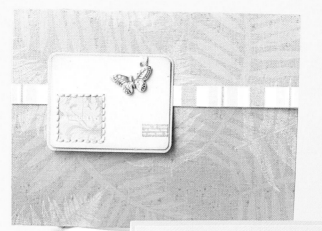

### Enjoy

Designer: Amber Crosby

SUPPLIES

**Textured cardstock:** (Leapfrog) *Bazzill Basics Paper* **Patterned paper:** (Sisters Floral/Red) *My Mind's Eye* **Stickers:** (Sarah Script alphabet) *American Crafts*; (epoxy couple) *Autumn Leaves* **Fibers:** (red stitched ribbon) *Making Memories*

**SPICE IT UP**

*Rotate the recipe for a quick variation on the design.*

**TIP A LA AMBER**

*Draw inspiration for colors and patterns from a simple accent. This card design and color palette were inspired by the vintage sticker.*

### Graduation Possibility

Designer: Nichole Heady

SUPPLIES

**Cardstock:** (sand, dark beige) **Textured cardstock:** (tan) *Die Cuts With a View* **Patterned paper:** (leaves, stripes from Vacation Papers collection) *Hot Off The Press* **Embossing powder:** (clear) *Stampin' Up!* **Accent:** (butterfly charm) *K&Company* **Fastener:** (hook and loop) *Velcro* **Rub-ons:** (sentiments) *American Traditional Designs* **Fibers:** (blue floss) *DMC*

**SPICE IT UP**

*Create a tri-fold card with the flaps overlapping where the recipe calls for a border strip.*

### Hello Girlfriend

Designer: Jana Millen

SUPPLIES

**Textured cardstock:** (lime, medium lime, bright pink, white) **Patterned paper:** (Ribbons from Wink collection) *Autumn Leaves* **Rubber stamp:** (Hello Girlfriend) *Hero Arts* **Dye ink:** (Black) *Stewart Superior Corp.* **Accent:** (sage button) *Making Memories* **Fibers:** (white, pink floss) *DMC*; (sage gingham ribbon) **Adhesive:** (pop-up dots) *Plaid*

**SECRET INGREDIENTS**

*Adhere the gingham ribbon to the cardstock. Then, stitch X's over the ribbon with floss.*

*Stitch on the cardstock block before adhering it to the card front so the stitching won't show inside the card.*

## Tropical Bon Voyage

Designer: JoAnne Bacon

SUPPLIES
**Cardstock:** (white) **Patterned paper:** (Passport Multi Stripe) *KI Memories* **Paper accents:** (green square) *KI Memories*; (blue, yellow flowers) *Prima* **Accent:** (green brad) **Rub-ons:** (Oda Mae alphabet) *Imagination Project* **Fibers:** (blue polka dot ribbon) *KI Memories*

## Sweet Baby Sundress

Designer: Wendy Johnson

SUPPLIES
**Cardstock:** (white, lavender) **Textured cardstock:** (Buttercream) *Bazzill Basics Paper* **Patterned paper:** (purple plaid) **Paper accent:** (baby dress) *Creative Imaginations* **Accents:** (purple round, yellow flower brads) *The Happy Hammer* **Fibers:** (white twill ribbon, white thread) **Fonts:** (Dreams) *www.twopeasinabucket.com*; (Arial) *Corel*

**TIP A LA WENDY**
*Replace the saying with "happy birthday"*
*for a fun card for a little girl.*

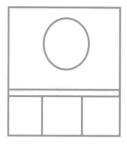

## Beautiful Be Mine

Designer: Wendy Johnson

SUPPLIES

**Textured cardstock:** (black, white) **Patterned paper:** (Tattered Red) *Scissor Sisters* **Accent:** (chipboard coaster) *Li'l Davis Designs* **Fibers:** (black gingham ribbon) *Offray*

INSTRUCTIONS

① Make card from black cardstock. ② Cut Tattered Red paper to fit top ⅔ of card front; adhere. ③ Cut small rectangle of white cardstock; adhere to bottom of card front. ④ Cut slit in card fold; thread ribbon through, wrap around card front, and knot. ⑤ Adhere coaster to card.

## Fabric & Flowers

Designer: Jana Millen

SUPPLIES
**Cardstock:** (white) **Textured cardstock:** (pink)
**Paper accents:** (yellow, white flowers) *Making Memories* **Accents:** (floral, stripe, polka dot canvas fabric) *Waverly*; (pink brad) *Making Memories* **Fibers:** (pink gingham ribbon) *Kate's Paperie*; (white thread)

## Sand, Sun, Surf

Designer: Alisa Bangerter

SUPPLIES
**Textured cardstock:** (yellow, light blue, dark blue) *Die Cuts With a View* **Accent:** (round metal concho) *Scrapworks* **Stickers:** (beach photos) *Cloud 9 Design* **Fibers:** (yellow polka dot ribbon) *May Arts*; (sheer yellow, yellow gingham ribbon) *Offray* **Tools:** (label maker) *Dymo*

### APPETIZING IDEA

*To make the word strip, run a strip of cardstock through the label maker to imprint the words. Then lightly sand the words to make them pop. Be sure to use colored cardstock with a white core so the words will show.*

## Little One Shaker

Designer: Amber Crosby

SUPPLIES
**Textured cardstock:** (Bazzill White) *Bazzill Basics Paper* **Patterned paper:** (Pink Bunnies, Pink ABC Blocks, Pink Victoria) *Anna Griffin* **Accents:** (pink shaker bubble) *Pebbles Inc.*; (pink beads) *Me & My Big Ideas* **Fibers:** (pink polka dot ribbon) *American Crafts*; (pink striped ribbon) *May Arts* **Font:** (Garamond) *Microsoft*

### ADD SOME FLAVOR

*Place a photo of the baby inside the shaker for a cute announcement.*

## Friends Forever Wall Décor

Designer: Dee Gallimore-Perry

SUPPLIES

**Patterned paper:** (Friendship Loops, Friendship Multi Stripe, Friendship Typing Test) *KI Memories* **Card pad:** (Designer Cards) *K&Company* **Paper accents:** (friendship quote, blue flower, pink circle, friends forever) *KI Memories* **Accents:** (lavender safety pin) *Making Memories*; (pink acrylic flower) *KI Memories*; (pink snap) *Target* **Fibers:** (blue striped, pink striped, green gingham ribbon) *KI Memories*; (light blue pearl cotton) *DMC* **Adhesive:** (pop-up dot) *Plaid*

MAKES ONE 5½" x 8½" WALL DECOR

### TIPS A LA DEE

*Use the back of a pad of cards or paper that has a hanging tab to make this wall hanging. Just cover it with patterned paper and embellish.*

*Replace one of the patterned paper panels with a photo of the friends to personalize the wall hanging.*

## 100% Girl

Designer: Nichole Heady

SUPPLIES

**Cardstock:** (ivory) **Textured cardstock:** (brown) **Patterned paper:** (Anuenue Flower) *Rusty Pickle* **Rub-ons:** (sentiments) *Die Cuts With a View* **Sticker:** (pink purse) *EK Success* **Tools:** (1¾" circle punch) *EK Success*; corner rounder punch

*a girl is innocence PLAYING IN THE MUD, beauty STANDING ON ITS HEAD, AND motherhood DRAGGING A DOLL BY THE FOOT. —ALAN BECK*

INSIDE

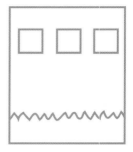

## Springtime Hello

Designer: Wendy Sue Anderson

**SUPPLIES**

**Patterned paper:** (HeatherRose/RoseBloom Linen from Homespun collection; Pretty Petals) *Bo-Bunny Press*
**Paper accents:** (butterfly, heart, flower) *Hot Off The Press* **Rub-ons:** (Heidi alphabet) *Making Memories*
**Adhesive:** (foam squares) *Making Memories*

INSTRUCTIONS

① Make card from HeatherRose/RoseBloom Linen paper. ② Adhere accents to top of card with foam squares. ③ Cut strip of Pretty Petals paper; adhere to bottom of card front. Zigzag-stitch along top of strip. ④ Apply rub-ons to spell "Hello".

## Bright Greetings

Designer: Heather D. White

SUPPLIES

**Patterned paper:** (Sunshine Yellow, Wide Stripe, Stripe from Beach Hut collection) *Fancy Pants Designs* **Dye ink:** (Van Dyke Brown) *Ranger Industries* **Paper accents:** (red, blue, orange flowers) *Fancy Pants Designs* **Accents:** (silver brads) *Making Memories* **Fibers:** (red gingham ribbon) *Making Memories*

## Patriotic Celebration

Designer: Wendy Johnson

SUPPLIES

**Cardstock:** (white) **Textured cardstock:** (Pomegranate) *Bazzill Basics Paper* **Patterned paper:** (Shabby Sky Blue Gingham) *Bo-Bunny Press* **Accents:** (star buttons) *Making Memories* **Rub-ons:** (alphabet) **Fibers:** (white rickrack) *Wrights:* (white floss) *DMC*

## Paisley Garden

Designer: Michelle Tardie

SUPPLIES

**Card:** (Orange from In Bloom) *Making Memories* **Patterned paper:** (Golden Delicious, Gala Plaid, Rome Paisley, McIntosh Bouquet from Cider Days collection) *Imagination Project* **Paper accent:** (yellow flower) *Making Memories* **Accents:** (black photo anchors; red, black brads) *Making Memories* **Rub-on:** (stitching) *My Mind's Eye* **Stickers:** (silver-lined epoxy squares) *Creative Imaginations*

### SPICE IT UP
*Flip the design to create a horizontal instead of vertical card.*

### TIP A LA MICHELLE
*To keep the photo anchors in place, adhere them down with mini adhesive dots before fastening with brads.*

### ADD SOME FLAVOR
*Change the flower accent to a leaf for a masculine card.*

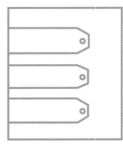

## You Did It

Designer: Sande Krieger

SUPPLIES

**Patterned paper:** (Circle Flowers from Dynamic collection) *Autumn Leaves*; (Kiwi Splatter) *Bo-Bunny Press* **Rubber stamps:** (Erosion alphabet) *Fontwerks*; (Buttons alphabet) *Duncan* **Dye ink:** (Brick) *Ranger Industries* **Paper accents:** (white mini tags) *Making Memories* **Rub-ons:** (Circus, Mixed alphabets) *Making Memories* **Fibers:** (orange ribbon) *May Arts*; (white thread)

INSTRUCTIONS

❶ Make card from Kiwi Splatter paper. ❷ Cut three 1½" x 3¼" tags from Circle Flowers paper. Trim three small squares from Kiwi Splatter; adhere to tag tops and punch hole in center of each. ❸ Stamp "Way to go" on mini tags; tie onto large tags with ribbon. ❹ Adhere large tags to card, folding ends over ½" and adhering to back of card. ❺ Stitch border around large tags. ❻ Apply rub-ons to large tags to spell "You did it".

## Happy Birthday Dad Bag
Designer: Wendy Johnson

SUPPLIES

**Cardstock:** (Peanut) *Bazzill Basics Paper* **Accents:** (Theodore fabric tags) *Making Memories;* (assorted round brads, brown acrylic sentiment) *Jo-Ann Stores;* (square copper brads) *All My Memories;* (copper D) *Hirschberg Schutz & Co.;* (chipboard A) *Rusty Pickle;* (twill D) *Carolee's Creations* **Stickers:** (White/Pearl alphabet) *All My Memories* **Fibers:** (brown striped ribbon, brown thread)

MAKES ONE 5¼" x 8¼" BAG

## Happy Birthday Mom
Designer: Michelle Tardie

SUPPLIES

**Card:** (Red from In Bloom) *Making Memories* **Patterned paper:** (Yellow/Orange Stripes on Worn) *Scenic Route Paper Co.* **Paper accents:** (orange tags) *Little Black Dress Designs* **Accents:** (yellow metal flowers) *Creative Imaginations* **Stickers:** (Curly alphabet) *Me & My Big Ideas* **Fibers:** (Butter twill ribbon) *Scenic Route Paper Co.*

## Little Boy Blue
Designer: Alice Golden

SUPPLIES

**Cardstock:** (Soft Blue from Baby Boy collection) *Deja Views* **Patterned paper:** (argyle, brushed from Baby Boy Papers & Pieces Tablet; Collage/Dreams from Baby Boy collection) *Deja Views* **Accents:** (blue buttons) *SEI* **Rub-on:** (sentiment) *Deja Views* **Stickers:** (Just Plain Simple alphabet) *Doodlebug Design* **Fibers:** (blue floss) *On the Surface* **Tools:** (sanding file) *Making Memories;* (corner rounder punch) *Creative Memories*

### APPETIZING IDEAS
*Sand the edges of the patterned paper for a subtle distressed effect. Round the corners of the three strips to soften the look.*

*Leave the bottom 1" of the patterned paper strips loose to add dimension to the card.*

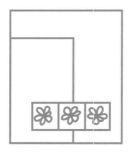

## Special Precious Dream

Designer: Angelia Wigginton

### SUPPLIES

**Cardstock:** (ivory) **Patterned paper:** (Thrifty Dots, Thrifty Harlequin from Thrift Store collection) *Autumn Leaves* **Dye ink:** (Van Dyke Brown) *Ranger Industries* **Accents:** (metal labels) *K&Company* **Stickers:** (canvas flowers) *Autumn Leaves* **Fibers:** (white thread)

### INSTRUCTIONS

❶ Make card from cardstock. ❷ Cut Thrifty Dots paper slightly smaller than card front. ❸ Cut smaller piece of Thrifty Harlequin paper; zigzag-stitch to Thrifty Dots. ❹ Cut strip of cardstock; ink lightly. ❺ Stitch strip to patterned paper block; adhere block to card. ❻ Attach stickers and metal labels to cardstock strip. ❼ Lightly ink edges of card.

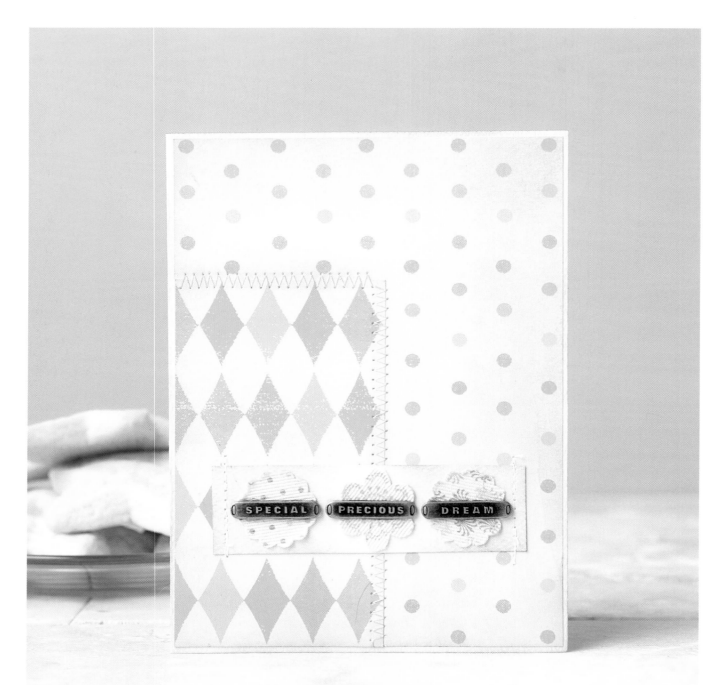

## Funky Party Invitation

Designer: Wendy Johnson

SUPPLIES

**Cardstock:** (mint green) **Textured cardstock:** (Icy Blue, Apricot, Sunshine) *Bazzill Basics Paper* **Patterned paper:** (Celebrate Petite Pop) *KI Memories* **Accents:** (yellow, pink metal-rimmed tags) *Making Memories*; (wish epoxy circle) *Target*; (flower brad) *Jo-Ann Stores* **Stickers:** (circle alphabet) *Jo-Ann Stores* **Fibers:** (green gingham ribbon) *May Arts*; (blue rickrack) *Wrights*; (white thread, yellow grosgrain ribbon)

### SPICE IT UP

*Think outside the recipe and turn a simple design element into a pocket for holding tags, a gift card, or a photo.*

## Pretty Petals Tag

Designer: Wendy Sue Anderson

SUPPLIES

**Patterned paper:** (pink gingham, pink/green stripe, green/white polka dot, green from Kate collection) *Making Memories* **Accents:** (pink plaid button, sheer flowers) *Making Memories* **Fibers:** (sheer polka dot ribbon) *May Arts*; (white thread)

MAKES ONE 3½" x 5" TAG

## Argyle Dad

Designer: Alisa Bangerter

SUPPLIES

**Textured cardstock:** (tan) **Patterned paper:** (Olive Bandana from Great Room collection, Billiard Argyle from Billiard Room collection) *Chatterbox* **Paint:** (Blue Heaven) *Delta* **Accents:** (tan fabric) *Junkitz*; (gold staples, brown buttons) *Making Memories*; (Rhyme Uppercase acrylic letters) *Heidi Swapp*; (olive green button) **Fibers:** (tan thread, white string)

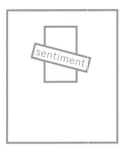

## Enjoy

Designer: Sara Horton

SUPPLIES

**Cardstock:** (white) **Textured cardstock:** (Hillary) *Bazzill Basics Paper* **Patterned paper:** (Pic-Nicky Table, Cayenne from Pic-Nicky collection) *Imagination Project* **Rubber stamp:** (enjoy from Great Words set) *Hero Arts* **Dye ink:** (Black) *Clearsnap* **Accents:** (gold staples) *Target* **Other:** money or gift certificate

INSTRUCTIONS

❶ Make card from Hillary cardstock. ❷ Cut Pic-Nicky Table paper to fit card front; adhere. ❸ Stamp sentiment on white cardstock; mat with Cayenne paper and staple to card. ❹ Slip money or gift certificate behind stapled piece.

## Pink & Brown Mother's Day

Designer: Nichole Heady

SUPPLIES

**Textured cardstock:** (Brown) *Die Cuts With a View*
**Patterned paper:** (Anuenue Flower) *Rusty Pickle*
**Transparency sheet; Accents:** (silver diamond brads) *Stampin' Up!* **Fibers:** (pink/brown striped ribbon) *Making Memories*; (pink thread, pink velvet ribbon) **Font:** (Avant Garde BK BT) *Microsoft* **Tools:** (scallop decorative-edge scissors) *Stampin' Up!*

## Look Who Is Two

Designer: Kathleen Paneitz

SUPPLIES

**Patterned paper:** (Cousins Stripe) *My Mind's Eye*; (Red & Cream Gingham) *Rusty Pickle*; (Keepsake Typing Test) *KI Memories* **Paper accent:** (rooster) *Westrim Crafts* **Rub-ons:** (red alphabet) **Font:** (CK Newsprint) *Creating Keepsakes* **Fibers:** (yellow ribbon) *Making Memories*

---

### SECRET INGREDIENT

*Personalize your ribbon with these simple steps.*
*1 Print sentiment on white paper. 2 Adhere ribbon over printed sentiment with repositionable adhesive and print again.*

## Ho, Ho, Ho

Designer: Lori Allred

SUPPLIES

**Cardstock:** (Chili) *Bazzill Basics Paper* **Patterned paper:** (Artichoke/Tarragon from Homespun collection; Cherrie Pie Dots) *Bo-Bunny Press* **Rubber stamps:** (Rummage alphabet) *Making Memories* **Dye ink:** (Van Dyke Brown) *Ranger Industries* **Accents:** (green wooden tag) *Over the Moon Press*; (copper snaps) **Fibers:** (twill ribbon) *EK Success*; (red grosgrain ribbon) *May Arts* **Adhesive:** foam tape

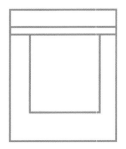

## Two Years

Designer: Sande Krieger

### SUPPLIES

**Cardstock:** (white) **Patterned paper:** (Thrifty Harlequin from Thrift Store collection) *Autumn Leaves* **Rubber stamps:** (Confidential alphabet) *Fontwerks* **Dye ink:** (Vintage Photo) *Ranger Industries* **Paper accents:** (paisley tag. striped tag) *Autumn Leaves* **Accents:** (pink chipboard number) *Heidi Swapp*; (pink brads) *Making Memories*; (pewter hangers) *Li'l Davis Designs* **Fibers:** (pink twill ribbon) *Scenic Route Paper Co.*; (brown polka dot ribbon, blue rickrack) *May Arts*

### INSTRUCTIONS

❶ Make card from Thrifty Harlequin paper. Adhere twill ribbon to card; ink edges. ❷ Cover chipboard stencil with paisley tag; replace number. ❸ Attach brads and hangers to top of chipboard; tie ribbon through hangers and adhere to card. ❹ Stamp "Mr & Mrs" on striped tag. Tie rickrack through tag and adhere to card.

## Enjoy the Journey

Designer: Linda Beeson

SUPPLIES

**Textured cardstock:** (Parakeet) *Bazzill Basics Paper* **Patterned paper:** (Thrifty Harlequin from Thrift Store collection) *Autumn Leaves*; (Key Lime Pie from Lollipop Shoppe collection) *BasicGrey*; (Blue Sky from Friends collection) *Junkitz* **Dye ink:** (Fuchsia) *Clearsnap* **Chalk ink:** (Orange) *Clearsnap* **Accent:** (red brad) *SEI* **Rub-ons:** (sentiment, circle tag) *Making Memories*; (cancelled postage mark) *Creative Imaginations* **Tools:** (circle punch) *EK Success*

**APPETIZING IDEA**

*Create a distressed look on all your papers by inking the edges.*

## Trust the Creator

Designer: Susan Neal

SUPPLIES

**Textured cardstock:** (Espresso) *Bazzill Basics Paper* **Patterned paper:** (Stucco Pattern, Stucco from Motifica collection) *BasicGrey* **Rubber stamps:** (Crackle Background) *Duncan*; (All I Have Seen) *Wordsworth* **Transparency sheet; Pigment ink:** (Sepia, Black) *Clearsnap* **Watermark ink:** *Tsukineko* **Accents:** (gold brad) *Making Memories*; (metal frame) *K&Company*; (mica) *Plaid* **Fibers:** (cream and black ribbon) *Making Memories*; (white chiffon, olive grosgrain ribbon) *Offray* **Adhesive:** (decoupage) *Plaid*

**SECRET INGREDIENT**

*Adhere the mica using decoupage. It is transparent and will adhere thoroughly to the paper.*

## Doggy Treats Container

Designer: Wendy Johnson

SUPPLIES

**Container:** (clear) *Provo Craft* **Cardstock:** (cream) **Patterned paper:** (Doggie Treats from Pet Tales collection) *Sticker Studio* **Color medium:** (brown chalk) *Craft-T Products* **Accents:** (black brads) *The Happy Hammer* **Sticker:** (bone) *Westrim Crafts* **Fibers:** (black thread) **Font:** (Bleached Blonde) *www.twopeasinabucket.com*

MAKES ONE 5" x 4" x 4" CONTAINER

**APPETIZING IDEA**

*Paper isn't the only surface sketches work on. Use them on plastic containers like this one, or on other surfaces such as wood boxes, plastic trays, glass, and more. The only limit is your imagination!*

# RECIPE 19

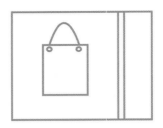

## Button Flower Thanks

Designer: Wendy Johnson

### SUPPLIES

**Cardstock:** (white) **Textured cardstock:** (Lemonade) *Bazzill Basics Paper* **Patterned paper:** (Venetian Stripes, Venetian Tiles from Blush collection) *We R Memory Keepers* **Accents:** (yellow button) *Jesse James & Co.*; (brown photo hanger, brown brads) *Daisy D's* **Fibers:** (brown grosgrain ribbon) *Michaels*; (white thread) **Font:** (Frazzled) *www.twopeasinabucket.com*

### INSTRUCTIONS

❶ Make card from white cardstock. ❷ Cut strip of Venetian Stripes paper; adhere to card. ❸ Adhere ribbon along edge of Venetian Stripes. ❹ Cut pink flower from Venetian Tiles paper; mat with Lemonade cardstock. Stitch around edges. ❺ Attach button, brads, and photo hanger to square; adhere to card. ❻ Print "Thanks" on white cardstock; trim into tag shape. Mat with Lemonade; attach to card with brad.

## Characteristics of Dad

Designer: Nichole Heady

SUPPLIES

**Patterned paper:** (Leonardo Harlequin Gold)
*Scenic Route Paper Co.*; (Scratched Orange)
*Karen Foster Design* **Specialty paper:** (brown
mulberry) *Stampin' Up!* **Accent:** (brass stick pin)
*K&Company* **Stickers:** (sentiment) *EK Success*
**Fibers:** (black twill ribbon) *Scenic Route Paper Co.*
**Font:** (Love Letter) *www.freetypewriterfonts.com*

### ADD SOME FLAVOR

*Type a list of your dad's most unique
characteristics and print them on
mulberry paper. Cut the words out and use them
to create a square block on your card.*

## A Purse for My Friend

Designer: Kathleen Paneitz

SUPPLIES

**Cardstock:** (white) **Patterned paper:** (Key Lime Pie
from Lollipop Shoppe collection) *BasicGrey*;
(Simply Worn Daisies) *Carolee's Creations* **Paper
accents:** (purse) *Westrim Crafts*; (friends tag)
*Making Memories* **Accent:** (silver jump ring)
*Making Memories* **Rub-ons:** (sentiment) *Making Memories* **Fibers:**
(pink ribbon) *Making Memories*

## I Wanna Be Just
Like You

Designer: Angelia Wigginton

SUPPLIES

**Textured cardstock:** (Beetle) *Bazzill Basics Paper*
**Specialty paper:** (Black Diamond velvet from
Grandpa's Attic collection; Debossed Daisy from
Granny's Kitchen collection) *SEI* **Paper accents:**
(frame, sentiment, tab) *SEI* **Rub-ons:** (wedding
sentiment) *Me & My Big Ideas*

### APPETIZING IDEAS

*Emboss plain cardstock or use embossed
cardstock for added texture and detail.*

*Use blue floral paper in place of velvet paper
for a more feminine version.*

*Use matching pre-made tags, squares,
and quote blocks for a quick card.*

sentiment

# Neighborhood Welcome

Designer: Wendy Johnson

### SUPPLIES

**Cardstock:** (red, white) **Patterned paper:** (blue splatter) *Keeping Memories Alive* **Rubber stamp:** (house from All God's Children set) *Stampin' Up!* **Dye ink:** (Black water-resistant) *The Angel Company* **Color media:** (watercolor pencils) Prismacolor, *Sanford* **Fibers:** (red and white gingham ribbon) *Offray* **Font:** (2Ps Chicken Shack) *www.twopeasinabucket.com* **Adhesive:** (foam tape) Scotch, *3M*; dots, glue stick **Tools:** (blender pen) *Dove Brushes*; sewing machine, computer and printer **Other:** white thread

### INSTRUCTIONS

❶ Make card from red cardstock.
❷ Cut blue splatter patterned paper slightly smaller than card front; machine-stitch to card. ❸ Stamp house on white cardstock; color with watercolor pencils and blend. Trim and mat with red.
❹ Print sentiment on white cardstock; trim and mat with red. ❺ Adhere house image to card with foam tape; adhere sentiment to card. ❻ Tie ribbon in bow; adhere to card with adhesive dots.

## Best Friends

Designer: Dee Gallimore-Perry

SUPPLIES

**Cardstock:** (Pear, Lilac, White) *Bazzill Basics
Paper* **Patterned paper:** (Lavender Mini Stripe)
*Kopp Design* **Rubber stamps:** (Friends from A
Little Love set) *Stampin' Up!*; (Background Script)
*Limited Edition Rubberstamps* **Dye ink:** (Basic
Black) *Stampin' Up!* **Accent:** (black label tape)
**Sticker:** (clear tag) *Clearly Yours, K&Company*
**Fibers:** (Celery ribbon) *Making Memories*; (lavender
gingham ribbon) *Impress Rubber Stamps*
**Adhesive:** (pop-up dots) Pop Dots, All Night
Media, *Plaid*; glue stick **Tools:** (label maker)
*Dymo*; scissors, sewing machine, hole punch
**Other:** white thread

## Striped Thank You

Designer: Wendy Sue Anderson

SUPPLIES

**Cardstock:** (white) **Patterned paper:** (Monarch
Stadium) League Collection, *Making Memories*
**Accent:** (Thank You 1) Jellies, *Making Memories*
**Sticker:** (Sentiments 2) Wonderful Words
Phrases, Déjà Views, *C-Thru Ruler Company*
**Fasteners:** (white eyelets) *Making Memories*
**Tools:** eyelet-setting tools, sewing machine, scis-
sors, ruler, craft knife **Other:** white thread

### TIP A LA WENDY SUE

*Do all machine stitching on a card before
adding any 3D embellishments. This will keep
the presser foot on the sewing machine from getting
stuck on the embellishments, and will also
make the stitching more even.*

## Friend, Teacher, Mom

Designer: Michelle Tardie

SUPPLIES

**Textured cardstock:** (Sunbeam) *Bazzill Basics Paper*
**Paper accents:** (mini brown bag) Paper Reflections,
*DMD, Inc.*; (Fresh Fabrics Red Gingham cutouts and
frame) This and That, *My Mind's Eye* **Stickers:**
(Family) Wordz, Art Warehouse, Danelle Johnson,
(Black Letters) Bits & Baubles Alphabets, *Creative
Imaginations* **Fasteners:** (black photo turn)
*Making Memories*; (black brad) *Karen Foster
Design* **Fibers:** (brown paper-wrapped wire)
**Adhesive:** (foam tape) Scotch, *3M*; glue stick
**Tools:** scissors

### TIPS A LA MICHELLE

*Trim pre-made frames and cutouts to create borders
in desired sizes for cards. Michelle trimmed the bottom
of a pocket cutout to create the strip under the flower.
She also adhered scraps of the pocket strip behind the
clear epoxy alphabet stickers to make them tan.*

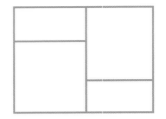

## Trendy Friend Four Flap

Designer: Wendy Johnson

SUPPLIES
**Cardstock:** (white) **Patterned paper:** (Cabana Stripes, Polka Dots, Paisley, Bias Plaid from Neapolitan series) *Collage Press* **Accents:** (brown brads) *Jo-Ann Stores* **Fibers:** (white string) **Font:** (Typo) *www.twopeasinabucket.com*

INSTRUCTIONS

① Make card from cardstock. ② Cut Polka Dots and Cabana Stripes paper to 4" x 2"; score each piece 1" from one end. ③ Fold flap over and adhere large flap to back of card. ④ Cut Paisley and Bias Plaid paper to 4" x 2"; score each piece 3" from one end. ⑤ Fold flap over and adhere small flap to back of card.

⑥ Punch four circles from reverse side of Polka Dots; adhere one to each flap. Attach brad to center of each circle. ⑦ Print "Friend" and heart on white cardstock. Trim into tag shapes and mat with reverse side of Paisley. ⑧ Punch holes in tags. Thread string through tag and attach to brads. ⑨ Wrap thread around brads to close flaps.

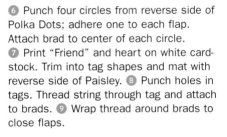

### SPICE IT UP

*Change an element of the recipe to create an interactive card like this one. Instead of using the squares on the card as flat pieces, use them to create a fun way to open the card.*

## Pink & Blue Belts

Designer: Lori Allred

SUPPLIES

**Textured cardstock:** (Bazzill White, Admiral) *Bazzill Basics Paper* **Patterned paper:** (Strawberries & Cream Polka Dot from Sherbet collection) *Making Memories* **Dye ink:** (navy blue) **Accents:** (Berry brads, Berry buckles) *Making Memories* **Fibers:** (pink/white/blue grosgrain ribbon) *Making Memories* **Adhesive:** foam tape

## Buggy Hello

Designer: JoAnne Bacon

SUPPLIES

**Cardstock:** (Spring Green) *Making Memories* **Patterned paper:** (gingham, small stripe, large stripe, plaid from MM Kids Ethan collection) *Making Memories* **Accents:** (green flower buttons) *Jesse James & Co.* **Rub-ons:** (Girly Girl alphabet) *Scrapworks* **Sticker:** (Dragonfly) *Westrim Crafts* **Fibers:** (blue rickrack, blue thread) *Making Memories*

### TIP A LA JOANNE

*To give buttons a finished or sewn-on look, tie ribbons or fibers through them and then adhere them to the card.*

## Tropical Envelope Birthday Wishes

Designer: Nichole Heady

SUPPLIES

**Paper:** (white) **Patterned paper:** (blue/yellow striped, peach/blue floral from Floral Prints Paper Stack) *Die Cuts With a View* **Accents:** (silver brads) *Stampin' Up!* **Stickers:** (Blueberry Block alphabet) *Creative Imaginations* **Fibers:** (hemp twine) *Stampin' Up!* **Font:** (CK Artisan) *Creating Keepsakes*

*Note: Envelope pattern on p. 54*

### SPICE IT UP

*Instead of the two smaller rectangles in the recipe, make a small envelope with coordinating discs and hemp twine. Each envelope opens to reveal wishes and dreams for the recipient.*

**ENVELOPES OPEN**

## Get Well Tag

Designer: Sara Horton

SUPPLIES
**Cardstock:** (White) *Die Cuts With a View* **Textured cardstock:** (Pink) *Die Cuts With a View* **Patterned paper:** (The Fifth Ad, Just in Jersey from Desperately Seeking Summer collection) *Imagination Project* **Rubber stamp:** (Little Prayer) *My Sentiments Exactly!* **Dye ink:** (Coal Black) *Clearsnap* **Accents:** (pink photo corners) *Heidi Swapp* **Fibers:** (black dotted, white ribbon) *Heidi Swapp*

MAKES ONE 6" x 3½" TAG

## Cheer, Noel

Designer: Marla Bird

SUPPLIES
**Patterned paper:** (Snowflakes from Be Merry collection) *My Mind's Eye* **Paper accents:** (words) *My Mind's Eye* **Color medium:** (brown chalk) *Pebbles Inc.*

**TROPICAL ENVELOPE BIRTHDAY WISHES**
Instructions on p. 53
Copy at 100%

**ENVELOPE PATTERN**
Cut 2 from peach/blue floral

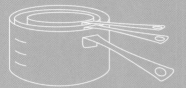

# CHAPTER 2

# Hearty Helpings

Bountiful in size and design, the recipes in this chapter

are two delicious sizes: 4" x 9" and 3⅜" x 6". These

recipes are so fun and versatile, you'll want to create

a second helping of cards!

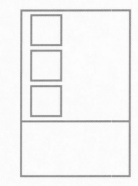

## Hello

Designer: Wendy Johnson

### SUPPLIES

**Textured cardstock:** (Windy) *Bazzill Basics Paper*
**Patterned paper:** (Kitchen Stripes) Granny's Kitchen, (Beatnik Diamond, Beatnik Rectangles) Beatnik Boy, *SEI* **Paper accents:** (circle metal-rimmed tag) *Avery Dennison*; (square metal-rimmed tag) *Making Memories*; (hello circle die cut) *KI Memories* **Accents:** (hello acrylic square) *KI Memories*; (hello label) *Making Memories* **Fasteners:** (light blue brads) *The Happy Hammer* **Fiber:** (green ribbon) **Adhesive:** (glue stick) **Tools:** (circle punch) *EK Success*; scissors, ruler

### INSTRUCTIONS

❶ Make card from Windy cardstock.
❷ Adhere Kitchen Stripes paper to lower 3½" of card. Adhere green ribbon to top of Kitchen Stripes; attach brads.
❸ Punch circles from Beatnik Diamonds and Beatnik Rectangles paper. Adhere to circle tags. ❹ Adhere hello accents to square metal-rimmed tag. Tie knot with green ribbon to tag. ❺ Adhere tags to card.

## To Love and to Cherish

Designer: Lori Allred

SUPPLIES

**Patterned paper:** (Venetian Lace, Heritage Stripe) Heritage Collection, *Making Memories* **Embossing powder:** (Platinum) *Stampin' Up!* **Stickers:** (wedding) Sticker Snapshots, *Pebbles Inc.* **Fibers:** (silver ribbon) **Adhesive:** (glue stick, foam squares) **Tools:** scissors, foam brush, heat tool, craft knife

### APPETIZING IDEAS

*Instead of wrapping ribbon around the entire card or adhering a small strip to the front, cut a small slit along the card crease using a craft knife. Tuck ribbon through slit and adhere to inside cover of card.*

## You & Me, Babe

Designer: Wendy Sue Anderson

SUPPLIES

*All supplies from Making Memories unless otherwise noted.* **Cardstock:** (ivory) no source **Patterned paper:** (Downtown Dot, Bias Cut Skirt) **Dye ink:** (Art Print Brown) Memories, *Stewart Superior Corp.* **Stickers:** (love, true love, you & me babe from love set) Like it is; (precious from baby set) Defined **Fasteners:** (heart brads) **Adhesive:** (foam squares); (glue stick) no source **Tools:** (scissors) no source

## Welcome Baby

Designer: Dee Gallimore-Perry

SUPPLIES

Cardstock: (Green Stripes) *My Mind's Eye*; (Bazzill White) *Bazzill Basics Paper* **Paper accents:** (die cut squares) *My Mind's Eye* **Rub-ons:** (welcome, baby) Simply Stated, *Making Memories* **Adhesive:** (glue stick) **Tools:** scissors

### SECRET INGREDIENTS

*Using double-sided paper adds endless variations to your projects.*

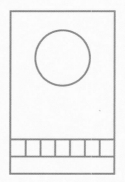

## Give Thanks

Designer: Wendy Johnson

### SUPPLIES

**Cardstock:** (ivory, orange)  **Paper:** (light green)
**Patterned paper:** (Green Plaid) *Patchwork Paper
Design*  **Paper accents:** (leaves, acorns, pumpkin die
cuts) *We R Memory Keepers*  **Font:** (Sunshine)
*www.twopeasinabucket.com*  **Adhesive:** (glue stick)
**Tools:** scissors, computer and printer

### INSTRUCTIONS

❶ Make card from ivory cardstock.
❷ Adhere light green paper to bottom of
card. ❸ Print "give thanks" repeatedly
on orange cardstock. Trim  and adhere to
top of light green. ❹ Adhere Green Plaid
paper to card. ❺ Adhere leaf and acorn
die cuts along bottom of card. Adhere
pumpkin die cut near top of card.

## Enjoy Your Travels

Designer: Ann Powell

SUPPLIES
**Textured cardstock:** (Lava) *Bazzill Basics Paper* **Paper accent:** (map tag)
Nostalgiques, *EK Success* **Rub-ons:** (Enjoy) Simply Stated Mini, *Making
Memories*; (your) **Stickers:** (Antique Alphabet) Real Life, *Pebbles Inc.* **Fibers:**
(black ribbon, fabric strips) **Adhesive:** (glue stick, foam square) **Tools:** scissors

## Aloha Greetings

Designer: Marla Bird

SUPPLIES
**Textured cardstock:** (Hillary, Lemonade) *Bazzill Basics Paper* **Patterned paper:**
(blue-green palm trees) **Color medium:** (brown chalk) **Stickers:** (alphabet)
**Fibers:** (braided raffia) **Adhesive:** (craft glue stick) Aleene's, *Duncan;* (foam
tape) **Tools:** (pineapple die cut, die-cutting machine) Sizzix, *Provo Craft/Ellison;*
craft knife, scissors

## Daisy Thanks

Designer: Wendy Sue Anderson

SUPPLIES

**Textured cardstock:** (light green, dark green, light yellow, dark yellow, light purple, dark purple, white) **Paper accent:** (flower) Embossible Designs, *We R Memory Keepers* **Stickers:** (classical alphabet) Architexture, *EK Success* **Fasteners:** (light purple eyelets) *Doodlebug Design* **Fibers:** (white crochet thread) **Adhesive:** (glue stick, foam squares) **Tools:** scissors, eyelet-setting tools

### ADD SOME FLAVOR

*Cardstock is often sold pre-packaged with several shades of the same color. All the colors match nicely, and it eliminates the guesswork in matching colors for your projects.*

## Amore

Designer: Sande Krieger

SUPPLIES

**Cardstock:** (red, white, black) **Rubber stamps:** (love, heart, floral, swirl from Wonderful Words set), *Stampin' Up!* **Pigment ink:** (Red) ColorBox, *Clearsnap* **Accent:** (pendant) I KanDee, *Pebbles Inc.*; (amore) woven labels, *Making Memories* **Fibers:** (black and white gingham ribbon) *May Arts* **Adhesive:** (glue stick, hot glue, hot glue stick) **Tools:** ½" square punch, scissors, hot glue gun

### APPETIZING IDEAS

*Create your own patterned paper by stamping various words or images in a repeating pattern. You'll have personalized paper to create unique cards.*

## Thanksgiving

Designer: Dee Gallimore-Perry

### SUPPLIES

**Cardstock:** (Terra Cotta) *Bazzill Basics Paper*
**Patterned paper:** (Shabby Black & Kraft, Pumpkin Bead Board/Splatter from Autumn collection) *Bo-Bunny Press* **Stickers:** (Thanksgiving images, sentiment) *K&Company*

### INSTRUCTIONS

❶ Make card from Terra Cotta cardstock. ❷ Cut Shabby Black & Kraft paper to fit card front; adhere. ❸ Cut half-ovals from Pumpkin Bead Board/Splatter paper; trim short rounded edges. Adhere to card. ❹ Apply stickers.

### SECRET INGREDIENT

*Whip up a batch of beautiful cards in minutes using dimensional sentiment stickers.*

## Bells and Petals Gift Tin

Designer: Heather D. White

SUPPLIES

*All supplies from K&Company unless otherwise noted.*

**Tin:** (quart paint) *Lowe's* **Patterned paper:** (Bordeaux Floral) **Specialty paper:** (Wedding Words Embossed from Bordeaux collection) **Accents:** (wedding bell metal charm, silver button brad); (silk daisy) no source **Fibers:** (lace trim) *Making Memories*

MAKES ONE 4¼" diameter x 4½" TIN

## Elegant Wedding Invitation

Designer: Wendy Johnson

SUPPLIES

**Textured cardstock:** (Dark Denim) *Bazzill Basics Paper* **Patterned paper:** (Gray Flowers & Vine from Elegant Wedding collection) *American Traditional Designs* **Vellum:** (white) *Stampin' Up!* **Photo; Fibers:** (blue ribbon) *May Arts* **Font:** (Commercial Break) *www.twopeasinabucket.com*

MAKES ONE 4½" x 6" CARD

Mr and Mrs Kenneth L Huntzinger
are pleased to announce
the marriage of their daughter

Krista Elaine
to
Gary Aaron Johnson

Son of Mr and Mrs Wells L Johnson
Saturday the seventh of January
Two Thousand and Six

Marriage Solemnized in the
Redlands California Temple

Reception                    Open House
Saturday Jan 7th             Saturday Jan 14th
8240 Keals Ave              714 N El Dorado Dr
Yucca Valley CA             Gilbert AZ
7:00-9:00 pm                7:00-9:00 pm

## Thanks Teacher Gift

Designer: Wendy Johnson

SUPPLIES

**Can; Cardstock:** (white) **Patterned paper:** (School Days Gold Star) *K&Company*; (Camping Green Plaid) *The Scrapbook Wizard* **Accent:** (leather apple) *EK Success* **Fibers:** (red grosgrain ribbon) *Offray*; (red thread) **Font:** (Rickety) *www.two peasinabucket.com* **Other:** pencils, gift shred

MAKES ONE 3" diameter x 5" CAN

### TIP A LA WENDY

*Fill the can with other gift items for your favorite teacher such as erasers, pens, a set of colored pencils, or scissors.*

## In Sympathy

Designer: Angelia Wigginton

SUPPLIES

**Cardstock:** (olive green) **Patterned paper:** (Denim Belle, Den Belle from Den collection) *Chatterbox* **Accents:** (olive green buttons) *Bazzill Basics Paper*; (black mini brads) *Making Memories* **Font:** (Patriot) *Autumn Leaves* **Fibers:** (white thread)

### TIP A LA ANGELIA

*Stitch the Den Belle semi-circles to the Denim Belle background paper and then attach the sewn piece to the card front. This will ensure the stitching doesn't show on the inside of your card.*

sentiment

# Friends Forever

Designer: Wendy Johnson

### SUPPLIES

**Cardstock:** (white) **Patterned paper:** (Pink Plaid) *Keeping Memories Alive*; (Green) *Making Memories* **Accents:** (friends, forever word tokens) *Doodlebug Design* **Sticker:** (flower) Quillettes Jolee's By You, *EK Success* **Fibers:** (white floss) *DMC* **Adhesive:** (glue stick) **Tools:** sewing machine, scissors **Other:** white thread

## INSTRUCTIONS

❶ Make card from white cardstock. ❷ Adhere Pink Plaid patterned paper to card front. Tear diagonally along edge of Green patterned paper; adhere to card. ❸ Stitch along edge of card and edge of tear. ❹ Adhere flower sticker. ❺ Adhere tokens. Secure with floss.

## Happily Ever After

Designer: Marla Bird

SUPPLIES

**Textured cardstock:** (Vanilla) *Bazzill Basics Paper*
**Accent:** (ring) Charmed Plaques, *Making Memories*
**Rub-ons:** (happily ever after from Wedding) Simply Stated, *Making Memories* **Fibers:** (white tulle)
**Adhesive:** (craft glue stick) Aleene's, *Duncan*
**Tools:** scissors

### TIPS A LA MARLA

*When adhering heavy items, use a thin, even layer of glue stick and weigh the accent down with several magazines or books to prevent warping.*

*Use different fibers such as ribbon or tulle to create borders on cards instead of cardstock.*

## Easter Greetings

Designer: Dee Gallimore-Perry

SUPPLIES

**Cardstock:** (Tangerine) *Bazzill Basics Paper*
**Paper:** (Green Tea Solid, Sunrise Solid) Collection I, *KI Memories* **Patterned paper:** (Citrus Plaid, Green Tea Graffiti) Collection I, *KI Memories*
**Paper accents:** (easter egg accent from Easter Mattes & More Kit) Dee's Designs, *My Mind's Eye*; (cardstock tag) *Making Memories* **Rub-ons:** (dates, numbers) *Autumn Leaves* **Stickers:** (black alphabet) Rat-A-Tat, Half-A-Bitties, *Provo Craft*; (powder vellum alphabet lowercase) Vellum Collection, *Mrs. Grossman's* **Fibers:** (pink gingham ribbon) *Impress Rubber Stamps* **Adhesive:** (glue stick) **Tools:** scissors, sewing machine **Other:** white thread

## M Is for Marriage

Designer: Sande Krieger

SUPPLIES

**Patterned paper:** (Pink Brocade, Cream Brocade) *Scenic Route Paper Co.* **Dye ink:** (Espresso) Adirondack, *Ranger Industries* **Paper accents:** (marriage) Defined, *Making Memories* **Accents:** (wood "M") *Li'l Davis Designs* **Stickers:** (baby girl) Straight Talk Stickers, *Pebbles in my Pocket* **Fastener:** (pink heart brad) *Creative Impressions* **Fibers:** (Vrown twill ribbon) *Scenic Route Paper Co.* **Adhesive:** (glue stick) **Tools:** scissors, sewing machine, hole punch **Other:** brown thread

## Mother of Mine

Designer: Wendy Johnson

sentiment

### SUPPLIES

**Cardstock:** (white) **Patterned paper:** (Plaid, Green, Daisy Clusters) Cottage Collection, *Chatterbox* **Accents:** (leather flowers) Jolee's Boutique, *EK Success* **Rub-ons:** (Heidi Black Large) Simply Stated Alphabets, *Making Memories* **Fibers:** (yellow grosgrain ribbon) *Making Memories* **Adhesive:** (glue stick) **Tools:** scissors, ruler

### INSTRUCTIONS

❶ Make card from white cardstock.
❷ Cut Daisy Clusters to 2" x 9", Green to 2" x 6", and Plaid to 2" x 3"; adhere to card. ❸ Adhere grosgrain ribbon and flowers to card. ❹ Apply rub-on sentiment to card.

### Sacred Tears

Designer: Ann Powell

SUPPLIES

**Cardstock:** (black) **Textured cardstock:** (Crimson) *Bazzill Basics Paper* **Vellum:** (striped) **Sticker:** (rose) Real Life, *Pebbles Inc.* **Fibers:** (green ribbon) *May Arts* **Font:** (Vivaldi) www.fonts.com **Adhesive:** (glue stick) **Tools:** scissors, computer and printer

**ADD SOME FLAVOR**

*The quote on the card reads: "There is a Sacredness in tears. They are not the mark of Weakness, but of power. They speak more Eloquently than ten thousand tongues. They are the Messengers of Overwhelming Grief, and of Unspeakable Love. —Washington Irvine"*

### Friendship Blooms

Designer: Lori Allred

SUPPLIES

Patterned cardstock: (Raspberry, Apple) Pure Juice Two-Textured, *Memories Complete* **Acrylic paint:** (Strawberries and Cream) Sherbet, Scrapbook Colors, *Making Memories* **Accents:** (safety pin, classic eyelet letter "F") *Making Memories* **Fibers:** (green, pink ribbon) *SEI* **Font:** (Pensmooth) www.*fontpoint*.com **Adhesive:** (mini dots) *Glue Dots International*; (glue stick) **Tools:** scissors, paintbrush

**APPETIZING IDEAS**

*Use metal letters to start sentences or bring attention to a specific word. Applying paint to the letter adds a personal touch.*

### Cherish Forever

Designer: Michelle Tardie

SUPPLIES

**Textured cardstock:** (Debossed Dots, Tea Towel) Granny's Kitchen, *SEI* **Paper accents:** (cardstock tags) Granny's Kitchen, *SEI* **Fibers:** (tan ribbon) *SEI* **Rub-ons:** (Cherish, Forever from Legacy set) Small Impress-ons, Danelle Johnson, Art Warehouse, *Creative Imaginations* **Adhesive:** (glue stick) **Tools:** scissors

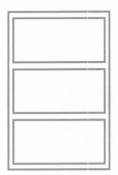

## Merry and Bright

Designer: Wendy Johnson

### SUPPLIES

**Cardstock:** (cream) **Patterned paper:** (Red Holly Jolly) PSX, *Duncan*; (Green Holly) *Anna Griffin*; (Antique Stripe) *K&Company* **Paper accents:** (star, present, heart die cuts) *We R Memory Keepers* **Fibers:** (red ribbon) *Li'l Davis Designs*; (green ribbon) *Offray* **Adhesive:** (foam tape) *3M*; (glue stick) **Tools:** scissors, ruler

### INSTRUCTIONS

❶ Make card from cream cardstock. ❷ Cut Red Holly Jolly, Green Holly, and Antique Stripe patterned paper to 3¼" x 2¾". Adhere to card front. ❸ Adhere ribbons to card. ❹ Adhere star, present, heart die cuts with foam tape.

## Girls' Night In

Designer: Sande Krieger

**SUPPLIES**
**Cardstock:** (Go-Go Green, Haute Pink) Hippie Chick, *SEI* **Patterned paper:** (Farout Flowers) Hippie Chick, *SEI* **Rubber stamps:** (alphabet) *Hero Arts* **Dye ink:** (Brown) ColorBox, *Clearsnap* **Paper accents:** (Hippie Frames, Tags, Labels) Hippie Chick, *SEI* **Fonts:** (Girls are Weird) *www.momscorner4kids.com*; (Franklin Gothic, Garamond, Humanst521 Cn BT, Juice ITC, Modern No. 20) *www.myfonts.com*; (French Script, Mistral) *www.fonts.com*; (Lesley) *www.fonttrader.com*; (Heritage) *www.scrapbook.com*; (Jenkins v2.0) *www.fontalicious.com* **Adhesive:** (glue stick) **Tools:** scissors, computer and printer

## Hello There

Designer: Wendy Sue Anderson

**SUPPLIES**
*All supplies from Making Memories unless otherwise noted.*

**Patterned paper:** (Slimming Stripe, Downtown Dot, Bias Cut Skirt) **Foam stamp:** (flower) no source **Dye ink:** (Sand) Memories, *Stewart Superior Corp.* **Acrylic paint:** (Strawberries & Cream) Sherbet, Scrapbook Colors **Sticker:** (hello there) no source **Fastener:** (antique brad) **Adhesive:** (glue stick) no source **Tools:** (scissors, paintbrush) no source

## Digital Dad's Day

Designer: Sande Krieger

**SUPPLIES**
Cardstock: (black, white) **Adhesive:** (glue stick) **Tools:** Adobe Photoshop CS, computer and color printer, scissors

### APPETIZING IDEAS

*This card was created with a software program! For complete instructions on how to make Digital Dad's Day, please visit our Web site at www.PaperCraftsMag.com/projects.*

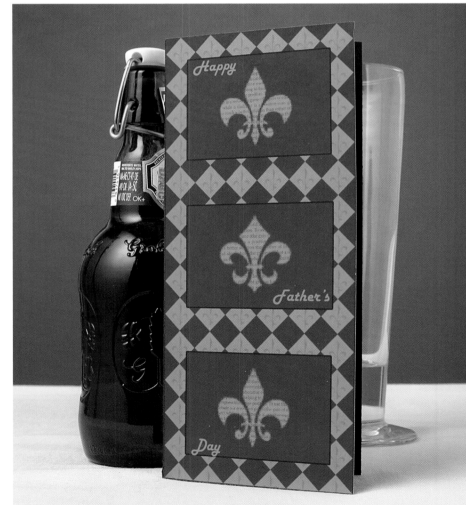

sentiment

○ ○ ○

# Missing You

Designer: Wendy Sue Anderson

### SUPPLIES

**Cardstock:** (brown) **Patterned paper:** (Da Vinci Script) *Design Originals*; (Antique Finish from Forget Me Not collection) *Daisy D's* **Vellum:** (white) **Stickers:** (clock, eyes, hands) *Design Originals* **Fibers:** (black gingham ribbon) **Font:** (AL Constitution) *www.twopeasinabucket.com* **Software:** (Word) *Microsoft*

### INSTRUCTIONS

❶ Make card from brown cardstock.
❷ Trim rectangles from Da Vinci Script and Antique Finish paper; adhere to card.
❸ Create text box in software program with black background and "Missing you" white text; print on vellum. Trim; adhere to card. ❹ Cut slit in card fold; thread ribbon through slit and wrap around card. Tie bow. ❺ Apply stickers.

## True Friend

Designer: Alice Golden

SUPPLIES

**Cardstock:** (Dotboard from Simply Chic collection) *American Crafts* **Patterned paper:** (Hippo Blankets) *We R Memory Keepers* **Accents:** (fabric labels, sentiment) *K&Company* **Fibers:** (Gidget grosgrain ribbon) *Strano Designs*

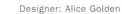

### SPICE IT UP
*Cover the inside of the card with solid cardstock if you prefer a subtler design.*

## Merry & Bright Gift Bag

Designer: Wendy Johnson

SUPPLIES

**Bag:** (red) *DMD, Inc.* **Patterned paper:** (Teal Distressed Wood from Studio K collection, Red Linen from Tommy's Toys collection) *K&Company*; (Maple Sugar/Vanilla from Homespun collection) *Bo-Bunny Press* **Stickers:** (snowflake and sentiment epoxy) *Autumn Leaves* **Fibers:** (tan gingham ribbon) *Creative Impressions* **Font:** (Bix Antique Script Hmk Bold) *Hallmark* **Tools:** (decorative-edge scissors) *Fiskars*

MAKES ONE 5¼" x 8½" BAG

## Miss You

Designer: Michelle Tardie

SUPPLIES

**Textured cardstock:** (Dark Black) *Bazzill Basics Paper* **Patterned paper:** (Pardon Me, Cayenne, Tomato Soup from Pic-Nicky collection) *Imagination Project* **Accent:** (gold flower) *Nunn Design*; (mustard brad) *Die Cuts With a View* **Stickers:** (Vintage Alpha Small alphabet) *Me & My Big Ideas*; (Distressed Typewriter Bubble Type alphabet) *Li'l Davis Designs*

### ADD SOME FLAVOR
*Apply epoxy alphabet letters to various dots on the Cayenne paper and trim them to create custom accents.*

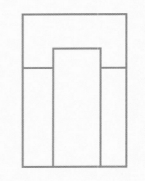

## Rustic Dad

Designer: Wendy Johnson

### SUPPLIES

**Cardstock:** (green, gray) **Color medium:** (brown chalk) *Craf-T Products* **Paper accent:** (striped tag) *BasicGrey* **Accents:** (silver brads) *Making Memories*; (My Type concho alphabet) *Colorbok* **Fibers:** (brown ribbon) *May Arts*; (white thread)

### INSTRUCTIONS

① Make card from green cardstock; chalk edges. ② Cut rectangle from gray cardstock; adhere to card. ③ Adhere ribbon. ④ Trim tag; stitch to card. ⑤ Attach conchos to spell Dad. ⑥ Attach brads.

## We've Moved

Designer: Alisa Bangerter

SUPPLIES

**Cardstock:** (tan) **Patterned paper:** (Lunch Sack/Barely Beige from Homespun collection) *Bo-Bunny Press*; (Herringbone, Swiss Dot, Corrugated, Vintage Paisley from Vagabond collection) *BasicGrey* **Accents:** (antique gold hinges) *Making Memories*; (antique brass nail head) *American Label & Tag* **Fibers:** (cream string) **Font:** (CopprplGoth Bd BT) *Microsoft* **Adhesive:** (pop-up dot) *Plaid* **Tools:** (mini circle punch) *Plaid* **Other:** sandpaper

### APPETIZING IDEA
*Print your new address info on Lunch Sack/Barely Beige paper and trim it to fit behind the door. Adhere a pop-up dot inside the door to add dimension.*

## Happy Birthday

Designer: Lori Allred

SUPPLIES

**Patterned paper:** (Happy Birthday Floral/Brown, Happy Birthday Floral/Pink) *My Mind's Eye*; (Maple Sugar/Vanilla from Homespun collection) *Bo-Bunny Press* **Paper accents:** (sentiment, definition tags) *My Mind's Eye* **Paint:** (Strawberries & Cream) *Making Memories* **Accents:** (antique gold hinges) *Making Memories* **Fibers:** (brown polka dot ribbon) *May Arts*; (pink sheer ribbon) *My Mind's Eye*; (white thread)

### APPETIZING IDEA
*Create a ribbon-embellished flap with the Happy Birthday title tag and hinges that lifts to reveal the birthday definition tag.*

## Happy Anniversary

Designer: JoAnne Bacon

SUPPLIES

**Cardstock:** (ivory) **Patterned paper:** (Green Vine, Love, Blue Stripe from In Love collection) *Sweetwater* **Dye ink:** (Chocolate Chip) *Stampin' Up!* **Paper accents:** (white flowers) *Prima* **Accents:** (brown brads) *Jo-Ann Stores* **Sticker:** (sentiment) *Jo-Ann Stores*

### TIP A LA JOANNE
*Ink the edges of color-coordinated patterned papers to tie the patterns together and provide dimension.*

INSIDE DOOR

INSIDE

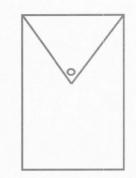

# Travel

Designer: Wendy Johnson

### SUPPLIES

**Cardstock:** (teal) **Patterned paper:** (Australian Map) *Rusty Pickle* **Accent:** (copper pebble word) *Jo-Ann Stores* **Fibers:** (brown thread)

### INSTRUCTIONS

❶ Make card from teal cardstock.
❷ Cut Australian Map paper slightly smaller than card front; stitch to card.
❸ Cut triangle from teal; stitch around edges. Adhere to card. ❹ Adhere pebble word.

## Flower & Belt

Designer: Jana Millen

SUPPLIES

**Cardstock:** (White) *Bazzill Basics Paper* **Patterned paper:** (Pretty Posies, Plot of Dots from Aunt Gerti's Garden collection) *SEI* **Accent:** (buckle) *KI Memories* **Fibers:** (green striped ribbon) *May Arts* **Tools:** (¼" circle punch) *Fiskars*

### APPETIZING IDEA

*Punch holes in the top of the card and thread ribbons through them to create a hinge. Stamp a sentiment under the flap.*

## Celebrate

Designer: Sande Krieger

SUPPLIES

**Textured cardstock:** (orange) **Patterned paper:** (Dizzy, Multi Squares on White, Light Green Brayer from Festivale collection) *Scenic Route Paper Co.* **Accents:** (yellow photo anchors) *Making Memories* **Rub-ons:** (assorted alphabets) *Making Memories* **Fibers:** (Strawberry, Pink Lemonade, Saffron, Lime twill ribbon) *Scenic Route Paper Co.*

### TIPS A LA SANDE

*Zigzag-stitch lengths of twill ribbon together before you cut them.*

*Use leftover rub-on alphabet letters to create a fun, funky look and save money.*

### SPICE IT UP

*Add additional design elements to dress up the basic recipe. Sande added tons of flavor with a festive sentiment block accented with rub-ons and twill ribbon.*

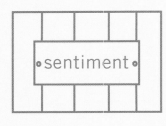

## Creepy Crawly Halloween

Designer: Wendy Johnson

**SUPPLIES**

**Cardstock:** (white) **Textured cardstock:** (Apricot, Parakeet) *Bazzill Basics Paper* **Patterned paper:** (Halloween Word/Stripe) *Pebbles Inc.*; (Spooky Petite Pop from Holiday collection) *KI Memories* **Dye ink:** (Basic Black) *Stampin' Up!* **Accents:** (Aloe Vera brads) *The Happy Hammer*; (felt spider) *Colorbok* **Font:** (Haunted House) *www.twopeasinabucket.com*

**INSTRUCTIONS**

❶ Make card from Parakeet cardstock. ❷ Cut rectangles from Halloween Word/Stripe and Spooky Petite Pop paper; ink edges. Adhere to card. ❸ Print sentiment on white cardstock; trim. Ink edges. ❹ Mat sentiment with Apricot cardstock; ink edges of Apricot. Adhere to card. ❺ Attach brads and spider.

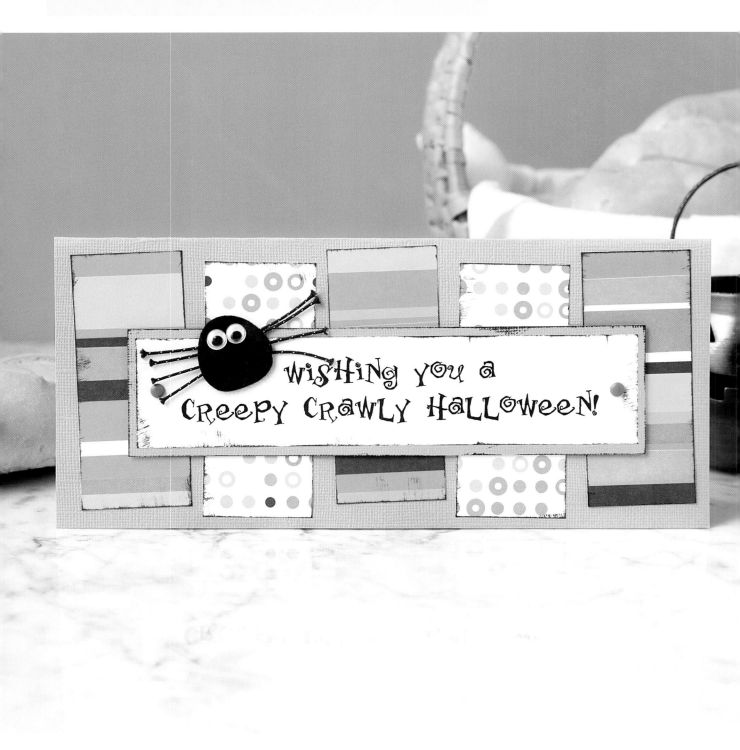

## Striped Thanks Tag

Designer: Sara Horton

SUPPLIES

**Cardstock:** (Black) *Die Cuts With a View* **Textured cardstock:** (Red) *Die Cuts With a View* **Patterned paper:** (Harlequaint from Hunky Dory collection, Yacht Harbor from Battery Park collection) *Imagination Project* **Paper:** (Ice from Flyby collection) *Imagination Project* **Accents:** (red staples) *Target*; (metal letter charms) *Making Memories* **Tools:** (¾" circle punch) *Family Treasures*

MAKES ONE 3½" x 6" TAG

## With Deepest Sympathy

Designer: Alisa Bangerter

SUPPLIES

**Cardstock:** (white) **Patterned paper:** (Runway Stripe from Avenue collection) *Making Memories* **Accents:** (forest green buttons) *Making Memories* **Fibers:** (light green sheer ribbon) *Offray*; (white string, thread) **Font:** (CK Wellington) *Creating Keepsakes* **Adhesive:** (foam squares) *Making Memories* **Tools:** (Hoki's Fern punch) *The Punch Bunch*

### APPETIZING IDEAS

*Punch fern leaves from patterned paper scraps to create color-coordinated accents.*

*Adhere the sentiment block to the card with foam squares for dimension.*

## Loving Thoughts

Designer: JoAnne Bacon

SUPPLIES

**Textured cardstock:** (Dark Butter) *Bazzill Basics Paper* **Patterned paper:** (Scarlet Bloom, Great Little Stripe, Great Room Floral, Chocolate Bandana, Scarlet Bandana from Great Room collection) *Chatterbox* **Dye ink:** (Chocolate Chip) *Stampin' Up!* **Accents:** (brown brads) *SEI*

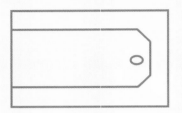

## Grandpa

Designer: Wendy Johnson

SUPPLIES

**Cardstock:** (white) **Patterned paper:** (Denim Argyle from Billiard Room collection) *Chatterbox* **Walnut ink:** (E-Z Walnut Ink) *Fiber Scraps* **Accents:** (canvas tag) *Creative Imaginations*; (antique metal charm) *Karen Foster Design* **Stickers:** (Sports Alphabet) *K&Company* **Fibers:** (antique ribbon) *Making Memories*

INSTRUCTIONS

❶ Make card from cardstock. ❷ Cut Denim Argyle paper to fit card front; adhere. Ink edges. ❸ Adhere canvas tag. ❹ Thread ribbon through metal charm; adhere to tag. ❺ Apply alphabet stickers to spell "Grandpa".

## Love

Designer: Susan Neal

### SUPPLIES

**Textured cardstock:** (Light Rosey, Dark Scarlet, Dark Burgundy) *Bazzill Basics Paper* **Patterned paper:** (Peppermint Stripe from Powder Room collection) *Chatterbox* **Rubber stamps:** (Just For You Text) *Impression Obsession*; (Love Vertical) *My Sentiments Exactly!* **Pigment ink:** (Vintage Sepia) *Tsukineko* **Accent:** (pewter decorative brad) *Making Memories* **Fibers:** (pink satin ribbon) *Bazzill Basics Paper*; (silver elastic cording)

### TIP A LA SUSAN

*Create a cardstock heart that's just the right size to cover the heart image in the letter O.*
*1 Stamp Love Vertical on Dark Scarlet cardstock.*
*2 Trim the stamped heart.*
*3 Turn over the heart and adhere it to the tag.*

## Love Defined

Designer: Sande Krieger

### SUPPLIES

**Textured cardstock:** (Stonewash) *Bazzill Basics Paper* **Patterned paper:** (Chocolate Tweed, Billiard Argyle, Denim Fleur from Billiard Room collection) *Chatterbox* **Transparency sheet:** (Love) *Creative Imaginations* **Dye ink:** (Vintage Photo) *Ranger Industries* **Accent:** (decorative brad) *The Paper Studio* **Rub-ons:** (French Quarter alphabet) *Advantus* **Fibers:** (blue and white fibers) *Chatterbox*; (brown ribbon) *May Arts*; (Fleur De Lis twill ribbon) *Autumn Leaves*; (white thread)

## Wish

Designer: Alice Golden

### SUPPLIES

**Textured cardstock:** (Bazzill White) *Bazzill Basics Paper* **Patterned paper:** (Dots with Flower from Inspire Me collection) *Heidi Grace Designs* **Accents:** (Wish tag, white eyelet) *Making Memories*; (green magnetic journal) *Karen Foster Design* **Fibers:** (Q.T., Savannah Wee ribbon) *Strano Designs*

### TIPS A LA ALICE

*Use the hole punch part of your eyelet-setting tools to create a clean hole in the ribbon for the eyelet.*

*Journal private notes such as birthday wishes, a love note, or favorite quotes in the magnetic accent. Adhere the journal to the card with repositionable adhesive if you want the recipient to be able to use it.*

INSIDE

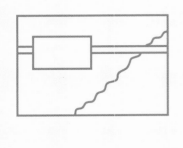

## So In Love

Designer: Alice Golden

### SUPPLIES

**Textured cardstock:** (Bazzill White, Licorice) *Bazzill Basics Paper* **Patterned paper:** (Love Stripes 2, XOXO from Love Collection) *Reminisce* **Color media:** (red chalk) *EK Success;* (Bubblegum Pink marker) *Marvy Uchida* **Sticker:** (sentiment) *Making Memories* **Fibers:** (Chloe grosgrain ribbon) *Strano Designs* **Adhesive:** foam tape

### INSTRUCTIONS

1 Make card from Bazzill White cardstock.
2 Cut Licorice cardstock to fit card front; adhere. 3 Cut rectangle from XOXO paper; adhere to card. 4 Cut rectangle from Love Stripes 2 paper; tear. Adhere to card. 5 Adhere ribbon; knot. 6 Apply chalk and marker to sticker. *Note: Refer to "Tips a la Alice" for best results.* 7 Adhere sticker to card with foam tape.

**TIPS A LA ALICE**

*Stickers with a matte finish generally produce the best results when colored; color glossy stickers with a dye-based ink.*

*Use the tip of a blender pen to pick up ink from the Bubblegum Pink marker, and color the sticker as desired. Add color and depth to the colored sections with red chalk and the blender pen. Then clean the blender pen and apply it to the colored sections to soften the colors and create a watercolor look.*

## Sugar & Spice

Designer: Heather D. White

SUPPLIES

**Textured cardstock:** (Baby Pink) *Bazzill Basics Paper* **Patterned paper:** (Dots, Daisies, Stripes from Joyful collection) *All My Memories* **Dye ink:** (Van Dyke Brown) *Ranger Industries* **Accent:** (fabric label) *K&Company*

## Mother's Day Gift Bag

Designer: Kathleen Paneitz

SUPPLIES

**Bag:** (brown) *EK Success* **Patterned paper:** (Plot of Dots from Aunt Gerti's Garden collection) *SEI*; (Daisy Tuner from Skinny collection) *Scrapworks* **Accents:** (decorative brads) *Making Memories*; (pink daisies tape) *Advantus* **Rub-on:** (barcode) *My Mind's Eye* **Stickers:** (Towering Type Glitter alphabet) *K&Company*

MAKES ONE 8" x 5" BAG

### SPICE IT UP

*Kathleen modified the recipe with an altered gift bag. She cut off the top of the bag, scored the cut edge, and folded it. The pink handles were made from the reverse side of the Daisy Tuner paper.*

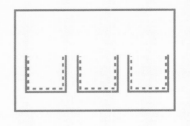

# Cupcake Wishes

Designer: Wendy Johnson

SUPPLIES

**Cardstock:** (Yellow) *One Heart...One Mind* **Textured cardstock:** (Pinecone, Lily White) *Bazzill Basics Paper* **Patterned paper:** (Blocked Scoop, Dotted Scoop, Target Scoop from Pink Lemonade collection) *One Heart...One Mind* **Accents:** (pink flower button) *Making Memories;* (yellow mini buttons) *Magic Scraps* **Fibers:** (white rickrack) *Wrights;* (white waxed string) *Close To My Heart;* (yellow, pink stripe ribbons) *May Arts;* (pink thread) **Font:** (Typo) *www.twopeasinabucket.com* **Adhesive:** (dimensional glaze) *Stampin' Up!* **Tools:** (paper crimper) *Fiskars*

## CARD BASE

❶ Make card from yellow cardstock.
❷ Cut Lily White cardstock slightly smaller than card front; stitch to card.

## CUPCAKES

❶ Cut trapezoids from Blocked Scoop, Dotted Scoop, and Target Scoop paper; crimp. Adhere side and bottom edges to card with dimensional glaze. ❷ Adhere rickrack. ❸ Cut three cupcakes from Pinecone cardstock. ❹ Print sentiment on white cardstock; trim and mat with yellow. Adhere to cupcakes. ❺ Embellish cupcakes with buttons and fibers as desired. ❻ Place cupcakes in pockets.

CUPCAKE TAGS

## Peach Pocket Trio

Designer: Lori Allred

SUPPLIES

*All supplies from My Mind's Eye unless otherwise noted.*

**Patterned paper:** (Floral Peach, Polka Dot Light Green from Spring collection) **Dye ink:** (orange) no source **Accents:** (decorative brads) *Making Memories* **Fibers:** (green grosgrain ribbon)

**ADD SOME FLAVOR**

*Embellish the tags with rubber stamps, stickers, or handwritten sentiments.*

## Mr. & Mrs. M

Designer: Nichole Heady

SUPPLIES

**Cardstock:** (red) **Patterned paper:** (Shades of Red) *Karen Foster Design* **Rubber stamps:** (Alphabits set) *Stampin' Up!* **Paint:** (White) *Delta* **Accents:** (red speckled mesh) *The Robin's Nest*; (white flower, folk heart eyelet shape) *Making Memories* **Rub-ons:** (Heidi alphabet) *Making Memories* **Sticker:** (Towering Type Glitter alphabet) *K&Company* **Fibers:** (Cajun ribbon) *Making Memories*; (white floss) **Tools:** (¼" circle punch) *Stampin' Up!*

## S-I-X

Designer: Alisa Bangerter

SUPPLIES

**Textured cardstock:** (Stonewash) *Bazzill Basics Paper*; (brown, white) **Vellum:** (striped from Boys pack) *My Mind's Eye* **Paper accents:** (striped pockets) *My Mind's Eye* **Accents:** (antique brass brads) *Making Memories*; (pennies, plastic animals) **Stickers:** (Textured Alphabet) *Sticker Studio* **Fibers:** (brown thread) **Font:** (CK Handprint) *Creating Keepsakes* **Other:** sandpaper

**APPETIZING IDEAS**

*Replace the contents of one or all of the pockets with flat wrapped candies, paper money, or gift cards.*

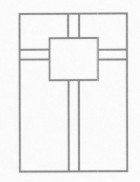

## With This Ring

Designer: Alice Golden

### SUPPLIES

**Cardstock:** (Natural) *Bazzill Basics Paper*
**Patterned paper:** (Midnight Elegance, Midnight Paisley, Kiss The Bride from A Day to Remember collection) *Bo-Bunny Press* **Accents:** (pewter charms) *Making Memories* **Sticker:** (Love) *Autumn Leaves* **Fibers:** (natural waxed linen twine) **Adhesive:** foam tape **Tools:** (emery board) *Making Memories*

### INSTRUCTIONS

❶ Make card from Natural cardstock. ❷ Cut rectangle from Midnight Paisley paper; adhere reverse to card. ❸ Cut rectangles from Midnight Paisley, Kiss The Bride, and Midnight Elegance paper; distress edges of two darkest rectangles. Adhere to card. ❹ Pierce sticker; thread twine through holes and charm. Knot. ❺ Mat sticker with Natural; mat with reverse of Midnight Paisley and distress edges. ❻ Adhere sticker to card with foam tape. ❼ Adhere pewter charms.

## Make a Wish Gift Bag

Designer: Wendy Johnson

SUPPLIES

**Bag:** (white) *Wal-Mart* **Textured cardstock:** (Bazzill White, Teal, Limeade) *Bazzill Basics Paper* **Patterned paper:** (Blue School Skirt) *Frances Meyer* **Accents:** (acrylic frame) *Making Memories*; (lime swirl buttons) *Jesse James & Co.*; (candle) **Rub-on:** (sentiment) *EK Success* **Fibers:** (blue gingham ribbon) *Offray*; (lime rickrack) *Queen & Co.*; (white thread)

MAKES ONE 5¼" x 8½" BAG

## Precious Boy

Designer: Ann Powell

SUPPLIES

**Cardstock:** (Outdoor Denim) *Close To My Heart*; (White) *Bazzill Basics Paper* **Textured cardstock:** (Apricot, Limeade, Pansy) *Bazzill Basics Paper*; (Nautical Blue Light) *Prism* **Accents:** (white brads) *The Happy Hammer* **Rub-ons:** (sentiment) *Making Memories*

## Adore Gift Bag & Tag

Designer: Heather D. White

SUPPLIES

*All supplies from Making Memories unless otherwise noted.*

**Bag:** (kraft) *DMD, Inc.* **Cardstock:** (white) no source **Patterned paper:** (Downtown Dot/Pink, Bias Cut Skirt/Brown from Cosmopolitan collection) **Accents:** (heart clips) **Stickers:** (sentiments) **Fibers:** (white)

MAKES ONE 5½" x 8½" BAG, AND ONE 2⅞" x 1⅞" TAG

# CHAPTER 3

# Savory Squares

Whip up your own perfectly square cards for every

occasion based on the plentiful recipes in this chapter.

sentiment

## Entwined Hearts

Designer: Wendy Johnson

SUPPLIES

**Cardstock:** (cream, green) **Patterned paper:** (Pink Espalier, Green Roses) *Anna Griffin* **Rubber stamp:** (Happy Anniversary from Greetings to You set) *Close To My Heart* **Dye ink:** (Mellow Moss) *Stampin' Up!* **Accent:** (metal hearts) Entwined Hearts, *Accent Depot* **Fibers:** (Celery ribbon, Perfect Pink cord) *Making Memories* **Tool:** scissors

MAKES ONE 5" SQUARE CARD

INSTRUCTIONS

❶ Make card from cream cardstock. ❷ Trim Pink Espalier and Green Roses papers; adhere to card. ❸ Adhere ribbon and cord to card. ❹ Trim square from cream; mat with green cardstock. Adhere to card. ❺ Adhere hearts to card. ❻ Stamp sentiment on card with Mellow Moss.

## Happy

Designer: Lori Allred

### SUPPLIES

**Patterned paper:** (Circus Stripe, Gumballs) *BasicGrey* **Dye ink:** (brown) **Acrylic paint:** (Nutmeg) Harvest, Scrapbook Colors, *Making Memories* **Accents:** (metal charm, flat marble) *Making Memories* **Rub-ons:** (Birthday set) Rub-Ons Mini, *Making Memories* **Sticker:** (Happy) Defined, *Making Memories* **Fasteners:** (Antique Copper brads) Mini Brads, *Making Memories* **Fibers:** (copper ribbon) Silly, *SEI* **Adhesive:** (dots) *Glue Dots International* **Tools:** (foam brush) Scrapbook Colors, *Making Memories*; scissors, paper-piercing tool, stylus

MAKES ONE 6" SQUARE CARD

## B My Valentine

Designer: Ann Powell

### SUPPLIES

**Cardstock:** (pink) **Acrylic paint:** (Strawberries & Cream from the Sherbet set, Hibiscus from Tropic set, Spotlight from Cityscape set) Scrapbook Colors, *Making Memories* **Paper accent:** ("b" from Poolside LC Jigsaw Alphabet) *Making Memories* **Accents:** (metal letters) Classic Eyelet Letters, *Making Memories*; (metal tag) Art Accentz, *Provo Craft* **Rub-ons:** (Evolution) Simply Stated Alphabets, *Making Memories* **Fibers:** (pink with white dots ribbon, pink variegated ribbon) *May Arts* **Adhesive:** (all-purpose craft glue) E6000, *Eclectic Products*; (foam tape) **Tools:** (foam brush, palette) Scrapbook Colors, *Making Memories*; scissors, wire cutters, stylus

MAKES ONE 6" SQUARE CARD

### SPICE IT UP

*Ann varied the placement of design elements to create a tighter focal point. Experiment by altering design colors, accents, and more to create something that fits your style instead of copying a design exactly.*

### TIPS A LA ANN

*Avoid over-mixing paint to achieve streaks and uneven coverage.*

*Mix two different paint colors with white in varying intensities on a palette before painting to make brush strokes visible.*

## Be Mine

Designer: Dee Gallimore-Perry

SUPPLIES

**Cardstock:** (Black) *Bazzill Basics Paper* **Patterned paper:** (Sommes, Harlequin Rouge, Le Monde Creme) French Collection, *7gypsies* **Rubber stamps:** (It's My Type Lowercase) *Ma Vinci's Reliquary* **Dye ink:** (Basic Black) *Stampin' Up!* **Walnut ink:** *FoofaLa* **Rub-ons:** (White Heidi) Simply Stated Alphabets, *Making Memories* **Fibers:** (black gingham ribbon) *Impress Rubber Stamps;* (khaki fabric strips) **Tools:** (L stencil) Warm White J-Q stencil, *Autumn Leaves;* (hole punch) ¼" rectangle, *Fiskars;* scissors, craft knife **Other:** sandpaper

MAKES ONE 5" SQUARE CARD

### APPETIZING IDEAS

*Shave the 3 open edges of the card with the blade edge of the scissors.*

*Sand the edges of the patterned papers before adhering them to the card.*

## Thanks, Teacher

Designer: Marla Bird

SUPPLIES

**Cardstock:** (Chili) *Pebbles in my Pocket* **Textured cardstock:** (Raven) *Bazzill Basics Paper* **Patterned paper:** (Lined Paper) *Karen Foster Design;* (I Will Not Chase Girls) *Rusty Pickle* **Rub-ons:** (Typewriter alphabet) *Autumn Leaves* **Stickers:** (Large Vowel Alphabitties, Middle School Stand-Outs) *Provo Craft* **Adhesive:** (craft glue) Aleene's Original Tacky Glue, *Duncan;* (glue stick) **Tools:** scissors, stylus, box cutter, needle **Other:** wood ruler

MAKES ONE 5⅝" SQUARE CARD

### TIPS A LA MARLA

*Wet the ruler before cutting it to keep it from splintering.*

*Place a paperweight on the ruler until the tacky adhesive is dry.*

## Mom

Designer: Michelle Tardie

SUPPLIES

**Cardstock:** (Celery) *Bazzill Basics Paper* **Patterned paper:** (Citrus Stripe) Collection I, *KI Memories* **Pigment ink:** (Black) ColorBox, *Clearsnap* **Stickers:** (Sophisticate alphabet) Danelle Johnson, *Creative Imaginations;* (Flowers & Insects) Brushstrokes, *Mrs. Grossman's* **Fibers:** (twine) **Tools:** scissors

MAKES ONE 4" SQUARE CARD

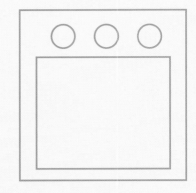

## It's a Zoo

Designer: Wendy Johnson

### SUPPLIES

**Cardstock:** (Home Companion) Made to Match, *American Crafts*; (kraft) **Patterned paper:** (Bloom Dot) Mary Engelbreit, *Creative Imaginations* **Color medium:** (black fine-tip pen) ZIG Memory System, *EK Success* **Paper accent:** (Animals Afloat) Paper Bliss, *Westrim Crafts* **Accents:** (Color Me Country buttons) Dress It Up, *Jesse James & Co.* **Fibers:** (paper wire) *MPR Paperbilities*, available at Wal-Mart; (white floss) *DMC* **Tools:** scissors, needle

MAKES ONE 4¾" SQUARE CARD

### INSTRUCTIONS

① Make card from Home Companion cardstock. ② Trim Bloom Dot paper; mat with kraft cardstock. ③ Draw stitch marks around edge of Bloom Dot. ④ Adhere paper accent to matted papers. ⑤ Stitch buttons to card. ⑥ Fasten paper wire around buttons; adhere matted papers to card over paper wire ends.

## Dump Truck

Designer: Marla Bird

**SUPPLIES**

**Textured cardstock:** (Root Beer) *Bazzill Basics Paper* **Patterned paper:** (Envelope Dark) *Real Life, Pebbles Inc.* **Transparency sheet:** *3M* **Accents:** (brown buttons) *Making Memories* **Sticker:** (Construction Zone) Stand-Outs, *Provo Craft* **Fibers:** (linen thread) **Adhesive:** (craft glue) Aleene's Original Tacky Glue, *Duncan*; (foam tape) **Tools:** scissors **Other:** sand

MAKES ONE 5½" SQUARE CARD

### APPETIZING IDEA
### HOW TO MAKE A SHAKER BOX

❶ *Place the dump truck sticker on the card.* ❷ *Create a box around the sticker from three layers of foam tape. Note: Be careful that the dump truck won't be covered when you add the border.* ❸ *Place the sand in the box.* ❹ *Trim the transparency sheet to cover the box and adhere a border of cardstock strips over the foam tape.*

## Smile

Designer: Ann Powell

**SUPPLIES**

**Cardstock:** (orange) **Patterned paper:** (Marmalade Block Party, Marmalade Bloomers) *Doodlebug Design* **Rubber stamp:** (flowers from All Occasion Celebration set) *The Angel Company* **Dye ink:** (Black Beauty) *The Angel Company* **Color media:** (watercolor pencils) *Derwent* **Accents:** (Marmalade buttons) *Doodlebug Design*; (acrylic word) Words & Phrases, Paper Bliss, *Westrim Crafts*; (slide mount) **Fibers:** (orange floss) *DMC* **Tools:** (blender pen) *Dove Brushes*; scissors

MAKES ONE 3¼" SQUARE CARD

## Friendship Daisies

Designer: Dee Gallimore-Perry

**SUPPLIES**

**Textured cardstock:** (Desert Sun) *Bazzill Basics Paper* **Patterned paper:** (Sunflower Double Plaid) Rustic Paper, *Kopp Design* **Dye ink:** (Black) Excelsior, *Stewart Superior Corp.* **Stickers:** (friend) Shabby Random Thoughts, *Bo-Bunny Press*; (daisies) Petal Pebbles, *Pressed Petals* **Fibers:** (black and white ribbon) *Making Memories* **Tools:** scissors

MAKES ONE 5" SQUARE CARD

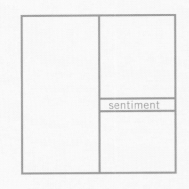

sentiment

# Baby Love

Designer: Wendy Johnson

SUPPLIES

**Cardstock:** (pink, white) **Patterned paper:** (pink gingham, pink dot) *Making Memories* **Color medium:** (black fine-tip pen) **Paper accent:** (pink daisy) Blossoms, *Making Memories* **Accents:** (white button) Dress It Up, *Jesse James & Co.*; (alphabet beads) *Darice*; (pink B flat marble) Tokens, *Doodlebug Design* **Sticker:** (black B) Time Saver Alpha Blocks, *All My Memories* **Fibers:** (Perfect Pink cord) *Making Memories*; (white rickrack, pink satin ribbon) **Tools:** scissors, hole punch

MAKES ONE 5½" SQUARE CARD

INSTRUCTIONS

① Make card from white cardstock. ② Trim pink gingham and pink dot papers; adhere to card. ③ Trim pink satin ribbon; adhere to card. ④ Adhere rickrack to card. ⑤ Write "Love" on white cardstock; trim into tag and punch hole. Thread cord through tag and button; knot. ⑥ Adhere flower to card; embellish with button and tag. ⑦ Mount letter sticker on pink cardstock; trim. Spell "baby" with accents.

## Cherish Forever

Designer: Michelle Tardie

SUPPLIES

**Cardstock:** (white) **Textured cardstock:** (Hazard, Thyme) *Bazzill Basics Paper* **Patterned paper:** (Green Tea Capri Stripe, Green Tea Lines, Sunrise Graffiti) Collection I, *KI Memories* **Paper accent:** (Citrus Circle Tag) Collection I, *KI Memories* **Accent:** (adhesive metal-rimmed tag) Tag Types Sticko, *EK Success* **Stickers:** (sentiments from Remember set) Defined, *Making Memories* **Fasteners:** (orange brads) *Making Memories* **Tools:** scissors

MAKES ONE 4" SQUARE CARD

## Gator Greetings

Designer: Wendy Sue Anderson

SUPPLIES

**Cardstock:** (white) **Patterned paper:** (Yikes Stripe Green, Multi-Dot Blue, Spatter Sky Blue) Cheri Strole Glossy Background Papers, *NRN Designs* **Stickers:** (gator and fish vellum) Cheri Strole Kidstuff, *NRN Designs*; (Uppercase Block Alphabet) Mary Engelbreit, *Creative Imaginations* **Font:** (Fairy Princess) www.twopeasinabucket.com **Tools:** computer and printer, scissors

MAKES ONE 6" SQUARE CARD

## Believe

Designer: Lori Allred

SUPPLIES

**Patterned paper:** (Winter Berries, Barn Red/Russet Red Fine Weave, Maple Sugar/Vanilla Poplin) Bo-Bunny Press **Dye ink:** (black) **Accent:** (metal word charm) Word Buckle, *Go West Studios* **Fibers:** (green ribbon) Savory Ribbon, *SEI* **Tools:** scissors, craft knife

MAKES ONE 6" SQUARE CARD

**TIP A LA LORI**

*Use a large stipple brush to ink card edges and you'll maintain more control of the color intensity than if you apply the ink directly from the pad.*

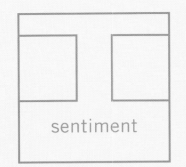

sentiment

## Basket of Easter Wishes

Designer: Wendy Johnson

SUPPLIES
**Cardstock:** (lavender, yellow, white) **Patterned paper:** (Baby Onesie) *Junkitz* **Accents:** (basket, egg buttons) *Blumenthal Lansing Co.* **Fibers:** (Butter twill ribbon) *Scenic Route Paper Co.*; (white thread) **Font:** (Kabel Book) *www.itcfonts.com* **Adhesive:** foam squares

MAKES ONE 5½" SQUARE CARD

INSTRUCTIONS
❶ Make card from lavender cardstock. ❷ Adhere two 2¼" x 3" pieces of patterned paper. ❸ Stitch along top, bottom, and inside edges of each piece. ❹ Punch hole through inside edge of each piece. Thread with ribbon and tie on button. ❺ Adhere eggs behind basket. ❻ Print sentiment on white cardstock with green ink; trim, mat with yellow cardstock, and adhere to card.

## Sending Birthday Wishes Your Way

Designer: JoAnne Bacon

SUPPLIES

**Patterned paper:** (Light Green Flowers, Mint Green Floral, Pink Paisley) *Sandylion* **Paper accent:** (yellow flower) *Prima* **Accents:** (Rosey, Sand tacks) *Chatterbox* **Rub-on:** (sentiment) *Karen Foster Design* **Fibers:** (light pink grosgrain ribbon) *Making Memories*

MAKES ONE 4½" SQUARE CARD

**APPETIZING IDEA**

*Re-create one motif on the patterned paper using dimensional accents. For this card, JoAnne assembled a flower to match a flower on the paper.*

## Tapestry for Mom

Designer: Jana Millen

SUPPLIES

**Cardstock:** (White) *Bazzill Basics Paper* **Textured cardstock:** (Rosey) *Bazzill Basics Paper*; (cream) **Patterned paper:** (Summer Days Paisley) *My Mind's Eye* **Dye ink:** (Van Dyke Brown) *Ranger Industries* **Accents:** (canvas flowers) *Autumn Leaves*; (antique copper brads) *Making Memories* **Fibers:** (tan gingham ribbon) *May Arts*; (cream thread) **Stickers:** (Just My Type alphabet) *Doodlebug Design* **Adhesive:** foam squares

MAKES ONE 5" SQUARE CARD

**APPETIZING IDEA**

*Use fabric embellishments and stitching to complement fabric-patterned paper.*

## Be Mine Box

**Designer: Alisa Bangerter**

SUPPLIES
**Patterned paper:** (XOXO Expressions) *Carolee's Creations* **Vellum:** (pink) **Box; Dye ink:** (Fired Brick) *Ranger Industries* **Watermark ink:** **Tsukineko Embossing powder:** (California Stucco) *Ranger Industries* **Paint:** (Crimson Tide) *DecoArt* **Dimensional glaze:** *JudiKins* **Accents:** (Poolside puzzle alphabet, red ribbon charm alphabet, silver brads) *Making Memories* **Fibers:** (pink organdy ribbon) *Offray*; (tan string)

MAKES ONE 5½" x 5½" x 3" BOX

### APPETIZING IDEA

*Cover the box with patterned paper; emboss the edges of each to add texture. Add a glossy finish to the puzzle letters by applying paint and a coat of dimensional glaze. To create a nice contrast with the glossy letters, emboss the negative puzzle pieces and box sides with textured embossing powder. Attach brads to the lid and box flap; tie closed with string.*

## Thanks for Your Support

**Designer: Nichole Heady**

SUPPLIES
**Cardstock:** (Perfect Plum, Ultrasmooth White) *Stampin' Up!* **Patterned paper:** (Far-Out Frames, Lavender Weave/Hunky Dory from Peachy Keen collection) *Keeping Memories Alive* **Rubber stamps:** (bra from Fashion Statements set, thanks from Everyday Flexible Phrases set) *Stampin' Up!* **Dye ink:** (Perfect Plum) *Stampin' Up!* **Watermark ink:** *Tsukineko* **Embossing powder:** (Silver Detail) *Stampin' Up!* **Accents:** (hook-and-eye fasteners) *Prym-Dritz* **Fibers:** (lavender stitched ribbon) *Making Memories*; (cream thread, white craft thread) **Tools:** scallop decorative-edge scissors

MAKES ONE 5" square CARD

### APPETIZING IDEAS

*Cut one 2" x 2½" piece of Far-Out Frames paper; mat it with Perfect Plum cardstock, sandwiching two loops of ribbon between layers on the right edge. Trim the right edge of the cardstock with decorative-edge scissors. Attach the hooks to the ribbon loops with craft thread; stitch the thread ends through the paper to form Xs. Create a second matted piece to go on the opposite side of the card; attach eyes to connect with the hooks.*

*Add dimension to the stamped bra piece by embossing the hanger to imitate the look of metal. Stamp the bra again on patterned paper, cut it out, and adhere it over the hanger. Trim and stitch the edges of the piece.*

## Just a Little Hello

**Designer: Sara Horton**

SUPPLIES
**Patterned paper:** (Harvest Small Daisies Chestnut, Sentimental Multi Dots/Stripe) *Scenic Route Paper Co.* **Fibers:** (Chartreuse twill ribbon) *Scenic Route Paper Co.* **Font:** (Essential) *www.twopeasinabucket.com* **Tools:** (1½" square punch) *Emagination Crafts*

MAKES ONE 4" square CARD

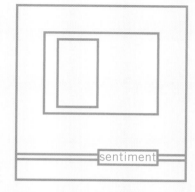

sentiment

## Potted Flowers

Designer: Wendy Johnson

### SUPPLIES

**Cardstock:** (green, cream, yellow, brown) **Patterned paper:** (Desert Blossom) Bitty Gone Big, *Provo Craft* **Color medium:** (brown chalk) Decorating Chalks, *Craf-T Products* **Accents:** (Country Tiny buttons) Dress It Up, *Jesse James & Co.* **Fibers:** (Celery ribbon) *Making Memories*; (twine) **Font:** (Dreams) *www.two peasinabucket.com* **Adhesive:** glue stick, foam tape **Tools:** (flower pot punch set) Floral Fantasy Collections, *McGill*; computer and printer, scissors, chalk applicator, needle **Other:** white thread

MAKES ONE 5½" SQUARE CARD

### INSTRUCTIONS

① Make card from green cardstock. ② Trim Desert Blossom paper; adhere to card. ③ Print sentiment on cream cardstock; trim. Mat with green. ④ Adhere ribbon near bottom edge of card; adhere sentiment block. ⑤ Trim rectangle from cream cardstock; chalk edges and tie ribbon. Mat with green. ⑥ Punch flowers, stems, and pot from cardstock (see photo); chalk pot edges and tie twine in bow. Stitch button to each flower. ⑦ Assemble and adhere potted flowers; adhere to cream with foam tape. ⑧ Adhere embellished rectangle to card.

## Snowman Christmas

Designer: Marla Bird

**SUPPLIES**
**Textured cardstock:** (Hillary) *Bazzill Basics Paper*
**Patterned paper:** (Christmas, Christmas Companion) Made to Match, *American Crafts*
**Sticker:** (snow girl) Christina Cole Stand-Outs, *Provo Craft* **Fibers:** (white sheer ribbon) *JKM Ribbon* **Tools:** scissors

MAKES ONE 5⅞" SQUARE CARD

### TIP A LA MARLA
*Save time and money by selecting patterned papers that include multiple design elements. Look for papers that include a variety of patterns, sentiments, and other card-making design essentials.*

### ADD SOME FLAVOR
*Use white sheer ribbon to soften the colorful, bold design of the card. The ribbon can also be used as a hanger to display the card throughout the Winter holidays.*

## Make a Wish

Designer: Dee Gallimore-Perry

**SUPPLIES**
**Cardstock:** (yellow) **Patterned paper:** (Blue Stripe, Cornflower Stroke) *My Mind's Eye* **Paper accents:** (candle, buttons, and sentiments die cuts from Celebrate Mattes & More) Dee's Designs, *My Mind's Eye*; (metal-rimmed tag) *Avery Dennison* **Tools:** (circle punch) *Emagination Crafts*; scissors

MAKES ONE 6" SQUARE CARD

## Congrats

Designer: Michelle Tardie

### SUPPLIES
**Cardstock:** (Beach) *Bazzill Basics Paper*
**Textured cardstock:** (Dark Black) *Bazzill Basics Paper* **Patterned paper:** (Bookprint) *Li'l Davis Designs* **Pigment ink:** (Black) ColorBox, *Clearsnap* **Stickers:** (alphabet) Scrappychic Vintage, *Me & My Big Ideas*; (grad cap from Glad to be a Grad) Cardstock Stickers, *Bo-Bunny Press* **Fasteners:** (black brads) *Karen Foster Design* **Fibers:** (black gingham ribbon) *Impress Rubber Stamps* **Tools:** scissors

MAKES ONE 5" SQUARE CARD

### TIPS A LA MICHELLE
*Spell the name of the recipient or graduation year next to the grad cap sticker with alphabet stickers or stamps.*

*Use the graduate's school colors as the color scheme for the card.*

## Welcome Home

Designer: Ann Powell

### SUPPLIES
**Cardstock:** (kraft) **Textured cardstock:** (Maraschino) *Bazzill Basics Paper* **Patterned paper:** (Liberty Plaid Navy, Freedom Stars Navy) *Daisy D's;* (Jolly Stripes/Red Plaid) Cutie Pie Flip Flop, *Keeping Memories Alive* **Rubber stamps:** (postage stamp from American Stamps set, America text from Mini Folk Flag set) *The Angel Company* **Dye ink:** (Black Beauty, Rustic Red) *The Angel Company*; (Old Photo) Distress Ink, *Ranger Industries* **Color media:** (watercolor pencils) *Derwent* **Paper accent:** (printed tag) Family Life Paper Tags, *Making Memories* **Fibers:** (red gingham ribbon) **Tools:** (blender pen) *Dove Brushes*; (decorative-edge scissors) Paper Edgers, *Fiskars*; scissors

MAKES ONE 5" SQUARE CARD

### APPETIZING IDEA
*Create custom patterned paper with sentiment stamps and coordinating ink. Ann stamped text from "America The Beautiful" on the red plaid paper to subtly reinforce the card's patriotic theme.*

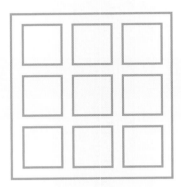

## Christmas

Designer: Wendy Johnson

### SUPPLIES

**Cardstock:** (gold, red) **Patterned paper:** (Brite Green) Perky Plaids, *Keeping Memories Alive* **Stickers:** (Christmas alphabet) Plus Mark, *American Greetings* **Fibers:** (gold cord) *Stampin' Up!* **Tools:** scissors

MAKES ONE 6" SQUARE CARD

### INSTRUCTIONS

❶ Make card from red cardstock. ❷ Trim Brite Green paper; mat with gold cardstock. Adhere to card. ❸ Mat stickers with red to spell "Christmas"; trim individually. ❹ Adhere matted stickers to card. ❺ Tie gold cord bows; adhere to desired stickers.

## Promise

Designer: Marla Bird

SUPPLIES

**Patterned paper:** (Britt) Made to Match, *American Crafts* **Accents:** (brown button) *Making Memories*; (white silk flower) **Rub-ons:** (future, devotion, promise from Wedding) Simply Stated Mini, *Making Memories* **Fibers:** (linen thread) **Adhesive:** (craft glue) Aleene's Original Tacky Glue, *Duncan* **Tools:** needle, scissors, stylus

MAKES ONE 5⅞" SQUARE CARD

### TIP A LA MARLA

*Remove the center of the silk flower in order to adhere it to the card and allow the petals to rise off the page.*

## Timeless Dad

Designer: Dee Gallimore-Perry

SUPPLIES

**Cardstock:** (Black) *Bazzill Basics Paper* **Patterned paper:** (Antique Harlequin) *Daisy D's Paper Co.*; (Pocket Watches) Chronicles, *Deluxe Designs*; ("Dad" letters cut from Weathered Cardstock 329) *Paper Loft* **Walnut ink:** *FoofaLa* **Fibers:** (black gingham ribbon) *Close To My Heart* **Tools:** (square punch) *Marvy Uchida*; scissors **Other:** sandpaper

MAKES ONE 5" SQUARE CARD

### TIP A LA DEE

*Buy walnut ink in a spray bottle or mix and store it in a bottle, so you can quickly age paper and tags. Keep mixed walnut ink in a resealable plastic bag or container for use in dipping or dunking embellishments.*

## Botanicals

Designer: Kathleen Paneitz

SUPPLIES

**Cardstock:** (pink, green, cream) **Dye ink:** (Coal Black) Designer Ink, *PrintWorks* **Stickers:** (Freedom Tags) Life's Journey, *K&Company* **Fasteners:** (silver mini brads) *Creative Impressions* **Fibers:** (black gingham ribbon) *Offray* **Tools:** (square punch) *Marvy Uchida*; scissors

MAKES ONE 5¾" SQUARE CARD

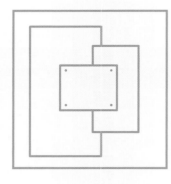

## Get Well Soon

Designer: Wendy Johnson

SUPPLIES

**Cardstock:** (white) **Patterned paper:** (Antique Barcode, Fresh Flower) Collection II, *KI Memories*; (Rose Dark Plaid) *Kopp Design* **Acrylic paint:** (Meadow) In Bloom, Scrapbook Colors, *Making Memories* **Paper accent:** (sentiment die cut) Soft Greetings Mod Blox, *KI Memories* **Accent:** (metal flower) Eyelet Charms, *Making Memories* **Fasteners:** (Rosey Tack) *Chatterbox*; (Splash brads) *The Happy Hammer* **Fibers:** (lavender gingham ribbon, white ribbon) *Making Memories* **Adhesive:** (foam tape) Scotch, *3M*; glue stick **Tools:** (foam brush) Scrapbook Colors, *Making Memories*; scissors, sewing machine **Other:** white thread

MAKES ONE 6" SQUARE CARD

INSTRUCTIONS

❶ Make card from white cardstock.
❷ Trim Antique Barcode paper; adhere and zigzag-stitch to card. ❸ Trim Rose Dark Plaid paper; adhere and straight-stitch to card. ❹ Trim Fresh Flower paper; adhere and zigzag-stitch to card. ❺ Adhere lavender ribbon to die cut. Tie white ribbon around lavender.
❻ Paint metal flower with Meadow; let dry. Fasten to die cut with tack.
❼ Adhere embellished die cut to card with foam tape. Attach brads.

## True Love

Designer: Kathleen Paneitz

### SUPPLIES

**Cardstock:** (white) **Patterned paper:** (Lemonade Blossom) Collection III, *KI Memories* **Paper accent:** (jewelry tag) *Avery Dennison* **Accents:** (love sentiment) Woven Labels, *Making Memories*; (wedding definition) Elements, *Daisy D's* **Rub-ons:** (sentiment) Itty Bitty, *Wordsworth* **Fasteners:** (flower wire brad) *Karen Foster Design* **Tools:** scissors, stylus **Other:** silver thread

MAKES ONE 4¾" SQUARE CARD

#### SPICE IT UP

*If you rotate the sketch, you can often double or triple the design possibilities. Kathleen was able to modify the design to include horizontal embellishments.*

## Miss You

Designer: Michelle Tardie

### SUPPLIES

**Textured cardstock:** (Dark Burgundy, Dark Fawn, Dark Violet, Walnut) *Bazzill Basics Paper* **Rubber stamps:** (Antique UC Alphabet) PSX, *Duncan* **Pigment ink:** (Pinecone) VersaColor, *Tsukineko* **Sticker:** (Forest Leaves) Pamela Woods, *Creative Imaginations* **Fasteners:** (Antique Copper mini brads) *Making Memories* **Fibers:** (jute) *Ace Hardware*; (twine) **Tools:** scissors

MAKES ONE 5" SQUARE CARD

## Father Defined

Designer: Lori Allred

### SUPPLIES

**Patterned paper:** (Big Den Plaid, Dark Den Circles, Den Paisley/Light Blue Weave) Den Collection, *Chatterbox* **Pigment ink:** (Brown) Distressing Kit, *Making Memories* **Accent:** (blue label tape) **Sticker:** (Father) Family Like It Is, *Making Memories* **Fasteners:** (Antique Copper mini square brads) *Making Memories* **Tools:** (personal label maker) *Dymo*; scissors

MAKES ONE 6" SQUARE CARD

## With Sympathy

Designer: Wendy Johnson

### SUPPLIES

**Cardstock:** (cream, white) **Patterned paper:** (Blue ABC Blocks, Green Plumes) *Anna Griffin* **Pigment ink:** (Vanilla) VersaColor, *Tsukineko* **Paper accent:** (Blue Roses die cut) *Anna Griffin* **Fasteners:** (Splash brads) *The Happy Hammer* **Font:** (Book Antique Italic) *Microsoft* **Tools:** stencil brush, scissors, computer and printer

MAKES ONE 6" SQUARE CARD

### INSTRUCTIONS

❶ Make card from white cardstock.
❷ Trim Blue ABC Blocks paper; mat with Green Plumes paper. Adhere to card.
❸ Print sentiment on cream cardstock; trim. ❹ Ink edges of cream cardstock with Vanilla; brush Vanilla on cardstock with stencil brush. ❺ Adhere flower die cut to card. ❻ Attach brads.

## Hi There

Designer: Dee Gallimore-Perry

SUPPLIES
**Cardstock:** (Cotton Candy Solid, Chocolate Solid from Eye Candy set) Collection III, *KI Memories*
**Patterned paper:** (Eye Candy Rhinestone Reverse from Eye Candy set) Collection III, *KI Memories*
**Paper accents:** (Casual and Cute font letters) Monograms, *My Mind's Eye* **Tools:** scissors, sewing machine **Other:** hot pink thread

MAKES ONE 6" SQUARE CARD

## Flower Pots

Designer: Michelle Tardie

SUPPLIES
**Cardstock:** (Buttercup) *Daisy D's* **Textured cardstock:** (Red Robin) *Bazzill Basics Paper*
**Patterned paper:** (Gingham Garnet) *Daisy D's*
**Stickers:** (Flowers) Time Saver Elements, *All My Memories* **Fasteners:** (silver mini brads) *HyGlo Crafts* **Fibers:** (Antique Red ribbon) *Li'l Davis Designs* **Tools:** scissors

MAKES ONE 5" SQUARE CARD

## Magnet Board

Designer: Marla Bird

SUPPLIES
**Textured cardstock:** (Root Beer) *Bazzill Basics Paper* **Patterned paper:** (Gumballs) *BasicGrey* **Specialty paper:** (Aluminum Metal Sheets) *Making Memories* **Walnut ink:** *7gypsies*
**Acrylic paint:** (Meadow, Poppy) In Bloom, Scrapbook Colors, *Making Memories*; (magnetic spray) *Krylon* **Font:** (Typewriter Rough) *www.clipart.com* **Adhesive:** (Shopping Bag book binding tape) *Making Memories*; (pop-up dots) **Tools:** (foam brush) Scrapbook Colors, *Making Memories*; computer and printer, scissors, magnet sheet

MAKES ONE 6" SQUARE CARD

### APPETIZING IDEAS
### HOW TO CREATE A MAGNET BOARD
*Create a whimsical magnetic board to display a custom message for the recipient. Here's how:*
❶ *Trim Aluminum sheet; spray with several coats magnetic paint.* ❷ *Dry-brush with Meadow and Poppy paints.* ❸ *Trim strips of book binding tape in half lengthwise; dampen with walnut ink. Adhere to Aluminum sheet edges.* ❹ *Print sentiments on coordinating patterned paper.* ❺ *Adhere sentiments to thin magnetic sheet; trim. Note: Old refrigerator magnets work well for the back of the sentiments.*

sentiment

## Forever Friends

Designer: Wendy Johnson

SUPPLIES
**Cardstock:** (red) **Patterned paper:** (Fuchsia Funky Swirls) Watercolor Collection, *Making Memories* **Accents:** (square, rectangle, and flower acrylics) Icicles, *KI Memories* **Fastener:** (white mini brad) *Impress Rubber Stamps* **Fibers:** (red gingham ribbon, pink gingham ribbon) *Offray;* (white ribbon) *Making Memories;* (red with white stripe ribbon) *Wrights* **Fonts:** (Falling Leaves, Flea Market) *www.twopeasinabucket.com* **Tools:** scissors, computer and printer, hole punch
MAKES ONE 5" SQUARE CARD

INSTRUCTIONS
❶ Make card from red cardstock. ❷ Print "forever" with Falling Leaves font and "friends" with Flea Market font on Fuchsia Funky Swirls paper; trim. Adhere to card. ❸ Adhere acrylic accents to card; set brad in flower center. ❹ Punch holes along top right edge of card. Tie ribbons through holes as desired.

## Happy Hanukkah
Designer: Nichole Heady

SUPPLIES

*All supplies from Stampin' Up! unless otherwise noted.*

**Cardstock:** (Night of Navy); (white) no source **Rubber stamps:** (Happy Hanukkah, menorah from Festival Fun set) **Dye ink:** (Night of Navy) **Accent:** (glitter) Dazzling Diamonds **Fibers:** (silver cord) **Adhesive:** (repositional) 2-Way Glue Pen, ZIG Memory System, *EK Success* **Tools:** (scissors) no source

MAKES ONE 4¼" SQUARE CARD

## Be Mine Forever
Designer: Kathleen Paneitz

SUPPLIES

**Cardstock:** (white) **Textured cardstock:** (Crimson) *Bazzill Basics Paper* **Patterned paper:** (French Script) Collage Papers, *DMD Inc.* **Accent:** (love sentiment) Woven Labels, *Making Memories* **Stickers:** (Skid Uppercase Letterz) Danelle Johnson, *Creative Imaginations* **Tools:** (square punch) Paper Shapers, *EK Success*; scissors

MAKES ONE 5" SQUARE CARD

## Happy Halloween
Designer: Wendy Sue Anderson

SUPPLIES

**Cardstock:** (light orange, white, black) **Textured cardstock:** (dark orange) **Patterned paper:** (Halloween Words) *Carolee's Creations* **Dye ink:** (Black) Memories, *Stewart Superior Corp.* **Accents:** (gold charms) Embellish It!, *Boutique Trims* **Fibers:** (black cord) *Making Memories*; (black polka-dot ribbon) *May Arts* **Font:** (Evergreen) *www.twopeasinabucket.com* **Adhesive:** (black foam squares, glue stick) **Tools:** scissors, computer and printer

MAKES ONE 6" SQUARE CARD

### APPETIZING IDEAS

*Distress the cardstock charm mats by shaving all sides with the blade edge of scissors and inking with black.*

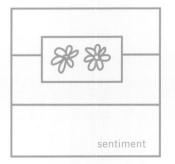

sentiment

## Halloween Fun

Designer: Lori Allred

### SUPPLIES

**Patterned paper:** (Black Beadboard from School collecton, Midnight Diamonds from A Day to Remember collection; Pumpkin Beadboard from Autumn collection) *Bo-Bunny Press* **Dye ink:** (black) **Paper accents:** (sentiment label, folder) *Making Memories* **Accent:** (paper clip) **Fibers:** (black diamond ribbon) *May Arts* **Adhesive:** foam squares

MAKES ONE 6" SQUARE CARD

### INSTRUCTIONS

❶ Make card from Black Beadboard paper. ❷ Cut 2" strips of Pumpkin Beadboard and Midnight Diamonds paper. Ink edges and adhere to card. ❸ Ink edges of folder, attach paper clip tied with ribbon, and adhere to card with foam squares. ❹ Wrap ribbon around bottom of front card flap; thread ribbon through holes in label; adhere with foam squares.

## Greetings Across the Miles

Designer: Alisa Bangerter

SUPPLIES

**Cardstock:** (tan speckled) **Textured cardstock:** (dark brown) **Patterned paper:** (Map from Vintage Travel collection) *Close To My Heart*; (Vintage Atlas) *Rusty Pickle* **Dye ink:** (Vintage Photo) *Ranger Industries* **Color medium:** (brown chalk) *Craf-T Products* **Accents:** (antique brass nail heads) *American Label & Tag Co.* **Sticker:** (airplane) *Me & My Big Ideas* **Fibers:** (cream string) **Font:** (CK Maternal) *Creating Keepsakes* **Adhesive:** foam tape

MAKES ONE 5½" SQUARE CARD

### TIP A LA ALISA

*Roughly ink the edges of all the paper pieces to enhance the vintage look. Make a clever border by attaching brads or buttons to the card corners, and wrapping them with string. Tie smaller lengths of string along the string border.*

## Have a Great Trip

Designer: Amber Crosby

SUPPLIES

**Cardstock:** (Natural) *Bazzill Basics Paper* **Textured cardstock:** (Tanner) *Bazzill Basics Paper* **Patterned paper:** (London Map from Life's Journey collection) *K&Company* **Accents:** (leather label holder) *Making Memories*; (silver brads) *Little Black Dress Designs* **Stickers:** (passport, road photo) *Pebbles Inc.* **Font:** (Garamond) *Microsoft*

MAKES ONE 6" SQUARE CARD

### SPICE IT UP

*Create a keepsake card for yourself or a fellow traveler. Decorate the card with a map and photos from your own vacation, and place the date and location of your trip in the label holder. Or, print a thank you message and give the card to someone who took care of your yard or pets while you were away.*

## Welcome, Neighbor

Designer: Wendy Johnson

SUPPLIES

**Cardstock:** (kraft) **Textured cardstock:** (Bazzill White, Lemonade) *Bazzill Basics Paper* **Patterned paper:** (HeatherRose/RoseBloom Linen from Homespun collection, Pretty Petals) *Bo-Bunny Press*; (Earth Green Vintage Vines) *All My Memories* **Specialty paper:** (Ivory Tusk, Kiwi textured) *Provo Craft* **Color media:** (brown chalk) *Craf-T Products*; (black pen) *American Crafts* **Accent:** (tan button) *Blumenthal Lansing Co.* **Fibers:** (cream floss) *DMC*; (white thread) **Font:** (Geeoh Hmk Bold) *Hallmark* **Die:** (heart) *Provo Craft/Ellison* **Adhesive:** foam squares

MAKES ONE 6" SQUARE CARD

### TIP A LA WENDY

*To give the card a homespun look, stitch the edges of the patterned paper strips on the card. Draw your own stitches and chalk the edges of the houses.*

## Love Flowers

Designer: Jana Millen

SUPPLIES

**Textured cardstock:** (Cream Puff, Dark Olive, Whirlpool) *Bazzill Basics Paper* **Patterned paper:** (Emblem, Thrifty Dots from Thrift Store collection) *Autumn Leaves* **Accents:** (Meadow alphabet) *Making Memories*; (cream buttons) *Junkitz* **Fibers:** (cream floss) *DMC*; (Scrollwork twill ribbon) *Autumn Leaves* **Tools:** (daisy punch) *EK Success*

MAKES ONE 6¼" SQUARE CARD

## Follow Your Bliss

Designer: JoAnne Bacon

SUPPLIES

**Cardstock:** (Natural) *Bazzill Basics Paper* **Textured cardstock:** (Dark Butter) *Bazzill Basics Paper* **Patterned paper:** (Dynamic Stripes, Floral Burst from Dynamic collection) *Autumn Leaves* **Paper accents:** (orange flowers) *Prima* **Accents:** (white brads) *Jo-Ann Stores*

MAKES ONE 5" SQUARE CARD

sentiment

## Santa Stops Here

Designer: Michelle Tardie

### SUPPLIES

**Cardstock:** (Blush Red Dark) *Prism* **Textured cardstock:** (Bazzill White) *Bazzill Basics Paper* **Patterned paper:** (Snowflakes, Stripes from Cool Holiday collection) *Creative Imaginations* **Accent:** (red brad) *American Crafts* **Stickers:** (sentiments) *Creative Imaginations*; (tag) *Creative Imaginations* **Fibers:** (blue grosgrain ribbon) *Bazzill Basics Paper* **Other:** sandpaper

MAKES ONE 5" SQUARE CARD

### INSTRUCTIONS

① Make card from Blush Red Dark cardstock. ② Adhere 5" x 2¾" piece of Stripes paper to bottom. Adhere Snowflakes paper to top right. Sand paper edges. ③ Adhere strips of Bazzill White cardstock over paper seams. ④ Affix tag sticker to card; punch hole through top of tag, going through all layers. Tie with ribbon. ⑤ Attach brad to To/From sticker and affix to tag. ⑥ Add remaining stickers.

## Birthday Boy

Designer: Linda Beeson

SUPPLIES
**Textured cardstock:** (Ciliega, Intense Kiwi) *Prism* **Patterned paper:** (Cabana Stripe from Sun Room collection) *Chatterbox* **Chalk ink:** (Prussian Blue) *Clearsnap* **Paper accents:** (alphabet strips) *The Weathered Door* **Accents:** (candle buttons) *Jesse James & Co.* **Stickers:** (Vintage Alphabet Large) *Me & My Big Ideas*; (black label tape) *Dymo* **Fibers:** (blue thread)

MAKES ONE 6" SQUARE CARD

## Girls Rock

Designer: Alice Golden

SUPPLIES
**Textured cardstock:** (Bazzill White) *Bazzill Basics Paper* **Patterned paper:** (Denim Stripes, Girl Talk Pink, Pink School Skirt) *Frances Meyer* **Accents:** (hot pink brad) *Karen Foster Design*; (denim, tweed flowers) *Making Memories*; (metal word tags) *K&Company* **Rub-on:** (sentiment) *Die Cuts With a View* **Fibers:** (orange floss) *Karen Foster Design*; (white thread)

MAKES ONE 6" SQUARE CARD

## Metallic Heart

Designer: Ann Powell

SUPPLIES
**Textured cardstock:** (black) **Patterned paper:** (Corrugated, Gingham Check, Scuff, Urban Dot from Vagabond collection) *BasicGrey* **Rubber stamps:** (Handwritten Lowercase alphabet) *Hero Arts* **Pigment ink:** (Basic Black) *Stampin' Up!* **Watermark ink:** *Tsukineko* **Embossing powder:** (Platinum) *Ranger Industries* **Paint:** (Asphalt) *Making Memories* **Accents:** (abalone shell button, lock washers) **Fibers:** (gray waxed linen thread) *Scrapworks* **Tools:** (½" circle punch) *Marvy Uchida*

MAKES ONE 5½" SQUARE CARD

### APPETIZING IDEA
*To make the metallic heart, cut it from cardstock, roughly coat it with watermark ink, and emboss.*

### TIP A LA ANN
*Purchase lock washers at a hardware store. Paint the washers black or leave them silver to match the embossed heart.*

### SPICE IT UP
*For a glossy finish, coat the letters behind the washers with dimensional glaze.*

## What Is Love?

Designer: Dee Gallimore-Perry

SUPPLIES

**Cardstock:** (White) *Bazzill Basics Paper* **Patterned paper:** (Light Pink Crackle, Pink Crackle, Red Crackle from Pink Crackle collection) *Creative Imaginations* **Transparency sheet:** (Love Black, Love White) *Creative Imaginations* **Rubber stamp:** (text circle from Conversation Dots set) *Hero Arts* **Solvent ink:** (Jet Black) *Tsukineko* **Accents:** (slide mount) *Creative Imaginations*; (pink daisy, white button) *Making Memories* **Stickers:** (paint chip sentiments) *Creative Imaginations* **Fibers:** (white thread)

MAKES ONE 6" SQUARE CARD

**APPETIZING IDEA**

*Decorate the plain button by stamping it with solvent ink.*

## Baby Shoes

Designer: Wendy Johnson

SUPPLIES

**Cardstock:** (Bazzill White) *Bazzill Basics Paper* **Patterned paper:** (Pastel Confetti) *Doodlebug Design*; (Green Garden) *Scissor Sisters*; (Buttercup Breezy Plaid) *The Paper Patch*; (Princess Pink Stripe) *Bo-Bunny Press* **Paper accent:** (baby shoes) *Me & My Big Ideas* **Stickers:** (Party Mix alphabet) *Doodlebug Design* **Fibers:** (light blue rickrack) *Target*

MAKES ONE 6" SQUARE CARD

**APPETIZING IDEA**

*To create a patchwork quilt look, adhere pieces of patterned paper to the card and stitch the edges of each piece. Accent one of the paper seams with rickrack.*

## Classy Purse

Designer: Wendy Johnson

### SUPPLIES

**Textured cardstock:** (Chantilly, Tickled Pink) *Bazzill Basics Paper* **Color medium:** (pink chalk) *Craf-T Products* **Accents:** (silver brads) *Making Memories*; (purse) *Meri Meri* **Fibers:** (black polka dot ribbon) *May Arts*

MAKES ONE 6" SQUARE CARD

### INSTRUCTIONS

① Make card from Tickled Pink cardstock. ② Adhere ribbon to center. ③ Adhere purse to piece of Tickled Pink. ④ Adhere to 4" x 3" piece of Chantilly cardstock; chalk edges. ⑤ Attach to card with brads.

## Love You

Designer: Angelia Wigginton

SUPPLIES

**Cardstock:** (Watermelon from Pieces of Me collection) *KI Memories* **Patterned paper:** (Nothing But Love from Pieces of Me collection, Hazard Flower from Together collection) *KI Memories* **Paper accent:** (heart tag) *KI Memories* **Rub-ons:** (alphabet) *K&Company*

MAKES ONE 5" SQUARE CARD

### APPETIZING IDEA

*To make an attractive gatefold card, cover the inside with patterned paper, then adhere paper strips to the inside edge of each flap. For a nice finishing touch on each flap, fold strips of patterned paper over the inside edges.*

## Trick or Treat Spider

Designer: Kathleen Paneitz

SUPPLIES

**Patterned paper:** (Wicked Stripes from Halloween collection) *Creative Imaginations* **Dye ink:** (Black) *PrintWorks* **Accents:** (white wooden frame) *Chatterbox;* (button spider) *Westrim Crafts* **Fibers:** (printed ribbon) *Creative Impressions;* (black/brown fibers) *Darice* **Other:** sandpaper

MAKES ONE 5" SQUARE CARD

### APPETIZING IDEA

*To create a haunting finish on the frame, sand the edges, then lightly rub the ink pad over the surface. Wrap fibers around the top of the frame and attach to the card, along with the spider.*

## Snowflakes All Around

Designer: Nichole Heady

SUPPLIES

**Cardstock:** (light blue, white) **Textured cardstock:** (White) *Die Cuts With a View* **Patterned paper:** (Snow from Text Prints Paper Stack) *Die Cuts With a View* **Rubber stamp:** ('Tis the season from Oh My Word! set) *Stampin' Up!* **Pigment ink:** (White) *Stampin' Up!* **Accents:** (snowflake brad) *Boxer Scrapbook Productions;* (Vintage Floral acrylic frame) *Making Memories* **Sticker:** (snowflake) *Creative Imaginations* **Fibers:** (light blue polka dot ribbon) *Zim's;* (white thread) **Adhesive:** foam squares **Tool:** 1⅜" circle punch

MAKES ONE 6" SQUARE CARD

### APPETIZING IDEA

*To make the snowflake accent, stamp the light blue cardstock, cut it out, and attach the brad. Affix the snowflake sticker to the brad. Adhere the accent inside the frame with foam squares.*

### SPICE IT UP

*Place your own photo inside the frame, instead of the snowflake accent.*

## Flower Tile

Designer: Jana Millen

SUPPLIES

**Cardstock:** (Licorice) *Bazzill Basics Paper;* (Be Bopn Blue, Spring Green) *SEI* **Textured cardstock:** (Lily White) *Bazzill Basics Paper* **Patterned paper:** (Dahlia from Smitten collection) *Autumn Leaves* **Accent:** (Smitten tile) *Autumn Leaves* **Rub-on:** (flower) *Junkitz* **Fibers:** (light green grosgrain ribbon)

MAKES ONE 5" SQUARE CARD

### APPETIZING IDEA

*Dress up the tile with the rub-on and ribbon length. Mat it with black cardstock to create a shadow effect.*

## Get Well Wishes

Designer: Marla Bird

SUPPLIES

**Cardstock:** (Sea Blue) *Bazzill Basics Paper* **Textured cardstock:** (Hillary) *Bazzill Basics Paper* **Patterned paper:** (The Great Outdoors Striped/Kiwi) *My Mind's Eye* **Accents:** (brown button, Honeydew label holder) *Making Memories;* (metal clip) *7gypsies;* (aqua beads) *Provo Craft;* (aqua wire, white silk daisy) **Fibers:** (linen thread) **Font:** (Angelina) www.momscorner4kids.com

MAKES ONE 6" SQUARE CARD

### APPETIZING IDEA

*To print the colored text piece for inside the label holder, see "Appetizing Ideas" for the Spooky Greetings card on p. 129.*

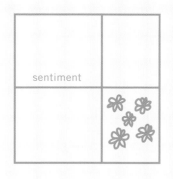

## Many Ways to Say Mother

Designer: Wendy Johnson

### SUPPLIES

**Cardstock:** (white) **Textured cardstock:** (Lime Green) *Die Cuts With a View* **Patterned paper:** (Mother from Text Prints Paper Stack) *Die Cuts With a View*; (Pink and Green Plaid) *The Scrapbook Wizard* **Accents:** (pink patterned, white brads) *Queen & Co.* **Fibers:** (white thread) **Font:** (Post Master) *Autumn Leaves* **Adhesive:** foam squares

MAKES ONE 6" SQUARE CARD

### INSTRUCTIONS

❶ Make card from white cardstock.
❷ Cut 2¼" x 3" piece each of Pink and Green Plaid paper and Lime Green cardstock. Attach brads to cardstock piece. Adhere pieces to right side. ❸ Cut 3¾" x 3" piece each of Mother paper and white; adhere to left side. ❹ Zigzag-stitch paper seams. ❺ Print sentiment on white; trim, mat with Lime Green, and adhere to card with foam squares.

## True Friendship

Designer: Wendy Sue Anderson

SUPPLIES

**Cardstock:** (Monarch from Avenue collection)
*Making Memories* **Patterned paper:** (Argyle Chic,
Rodeo Drive Dot from Avenue collection) *Making
Memories* **Rubber stamp:** (You're the Best from
All Occasion set) *Making Memories* **Dye ink:**
(Sand) *Stewart Superior Corp.* **Paper accent:**
(Friendship tag) *Making Memories* **Fibers:** (white
thread) **Adhesive:** foam squares

MAKES ONE 5¾" SQUARE CARD

## Happy 4 You

Designer: Linda Beeson

SUPPLIES

**Textured cardstock:** (Maraschino) *Bazzill Basics
Paper* **Patterned paper:** (Citrus Lines, Yellow
Circle Paisley) *The Scrapbook Wizard* **Accents:**
(blue flower buttons) *Impress Rubber Stamps*
**Stickers:** (Jumbo Letter alphabet) *Chatterbox*;
(Sea Horse alphabet) *Doodlebug Design* **Fibers:**
(blue striped ribbon, white thread)

MAKES ONE 5½" SQUARE CARD

## Happy Hanukkah

Designer: Michelle Tardie

SUPPLIES

**Textured cardstock:** (Dark Fawn) *Bazzill Basics
Paper*; (Suede Brown Medium) *Prism* **Patterned
paper:** (Brown Floral from Chandler collection)
*DeNami Design* **Pigment ink:** (Black) *Clearsnap*
**Accents:** (tan eyelets) *Eyelet Outlet* **Stickers:**
(dreidel, sentiment) *Scrapmandu* **Fibers:** (sage
green satin ribbon) *Offray*

MAKES ONE 4" SQUARE CARD

### TIP A LA MICHELLE

*To make the overlapping gatefold card, cut a
10½" x 4" strip of Suede Brown Medium
cardstock. Score and fold 4" from the right side,
and 2½" from the left side. Adhere cardstock and
paper pieces to both flaps; ink edges and add
stickers. Attach eyelets and tie card closed.*

## New Year's Countdown Party Invitation

Designer: Kathleen Paneitz

SUPPLIES

**Textured cardstock:** (Orange) *Die Cuts With a View* **Patterned paper:** (Corrugated from Vagabond collection) *BasicGrey*; (Celebrate Number Crunch) *KI Memories* **Paper accent:** (white tag) *Avery* **Accents:** (sentiment labels; Sky snap) *Making Memories* **Font:** (Outdoors) *Autumn Leaves* **Other:** sandpaper

MAKES ONE 4½" SQUARE CARD

## "M" Is for Mother

Designer: Dee Gallimore-Perry

SUPPLIES

**Cardstock:** (White) *Bazzill Basics Paper* **Patterned paper:** (Picnic Quad/Green Floral) *All My Memories* **Paper accents:** (definition) *Embellish It!*; (Mother tag) *Autumn Leaves* **Accents:** (Tangerine brad, Fuchsia safety pin) *Making Memories*; (Regal Red snaps) *Cloud 9 Design*; (red brad) **Rubons:** (Providence alphabet) *Making Memories* **Fibers:** (red gingham ribbon) *KI Memories*; (lime green polka dot ribbon) *American Crafts*; (Lily White rickrack) *Doodlebug Design*, (white string) **Other:** sandpaper

MAKES ONE 6" SQUARE CARD

INVITATION BACK

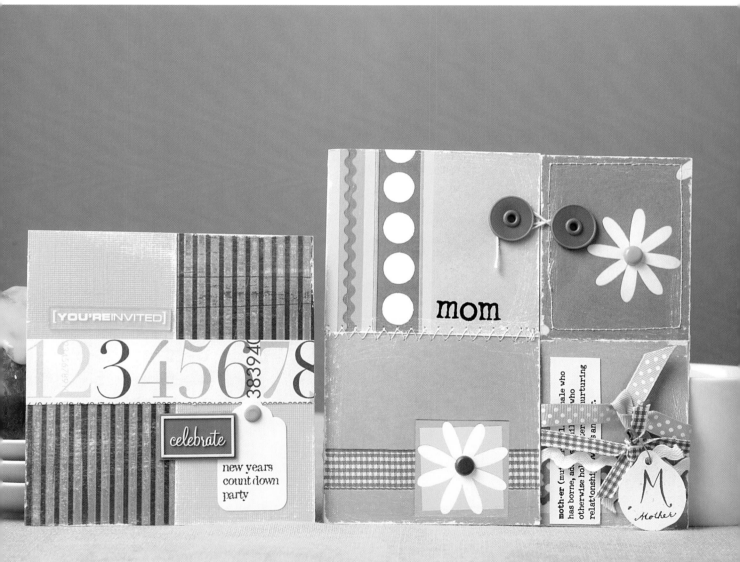

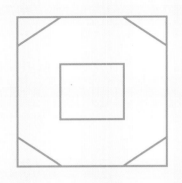

## Friends

Designer: Michelle Tardie

**SUPPLIES**

**Patterned paper:** (Happy Day Polka Dot/Blue) *My Mind's Eye* **Paper accents:** (sentiment) *My Mind's Eye*; (blue flower) *Prima* **Accent:** (blue brad) *American Crafts* **Adhesive:** foam tape **Tools:** (1½" square punch) *Marvy Uchida*

MAKES ONE 4" SQUARE CARD

**INSTRUCTIONS**

① Make card from Happy Day Polka Dot paper. ② Punch two squares from Blue paper; cut in half diagonally and adhere to corners of card front. ③ Attach flower to sentiment with brad. Adhere to card with foam tape.

## Congrats on Your New House

Designer: Susan Neal

SUPPLIES

**Cardstock:** (Black, Natural) *Bazzill Basics Paper* **Textured cardstock:** (Cocoa Butter) *Bazzill Basics Paper* **Patterned paper:** (Butter Bloom from Great Room collection) *Chatterbox* **Dye ink:** (Tea Dye) *Ranger Industries* **Accents:** (metal key) *Hirschberg Schutz & Co.*; (silver wire) **Font:** (Babe Bamboo) *www.fontpile.com* **Die:** (Home Sweet Home #2) *Provo Craft/Ellison*

MAKES ONE 5" SQUARE CARD

**SECRET INGREDIENTS**
*Create classy photo corners with ease. Simply cut Black cardstock squares in half. Cut thin strips of Cocoa Butter cardstock, ink the edges, and adhere to the photo corners.*

## To the New Parents-to-Be

Designer: Wendy Sue Anderson

SUPPLIES

**Textured cardstock:** (Yellow) *Die Cuts With a View* **Patterned paper:** (Baby from Text Prints Paper Stack) *Die Cuts With a View* **Accents:** (bib charm) *K&Company*; (pastel green, pastel yellow safety pins) *K&Company* **Fibers:** (light green ribbon) *K&Company*; (white thread) **Font:** (Flea Market) *www.twopeasinabucket.com*

MAKES ONE 5" SQUARE CARD

## A Big Hello

Designer: Wendy Johnson

SUPPLIES

**Cardstock:** (Pink, Yellow) *One Heart . . . One Mind* **Patterned paper:** (Polka Dot) *One Heart . . . One Mind* **Accents:** (yellow buttons) *Jesse James & Co.*; (wood alphabet) *Wal-Mart* **Stickers:** (square with pink border) *One Heart . . . One Mind* **Fibers:** (white floss) *DMC*; (pink thread)

MAKES ONE 6" SQUARE CARD

**TIP A LA WENDY**
*Thread always makes a card look polished. Stitch the edges of the matted Hello square with pink thread.*

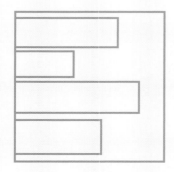

## For My Friend

Designer: Amber Crosby

### SUPPLIES

**Cardstock:** (Natural) *Bazzill Basics Paper*
**Textured cardstock:** (Parakeet) *Bazzill Basics Paper* **Patterned paper:** (Dorm Campus Flower, Dorm Plaid) *Chatterbox* **Accents:** (epoxy sentiment tiles) *KI Memories*; (copper brads) *Impress Rubber Stamps* **Fibers:** (orange grosgrain ribbon) *Fibers by the Yard* **Font:** (CK Script) *Creating Keepsakes*

MAKES ONE 6" SQUARE CARD

### INSTRUCTIONS

❶ Make card from Parakeet cardstock. ❷ Cover card front with Dorm Campus Flower paper. ❸ Cut four 1¼" strips of Dorm Plaid paper. Trim to various lengths and adhere to card. ❹ Adhere ribbon to longest strip. Print sentiment on Natural cardstock with orange ink; trim, attach brads, and adhere over ribbon. ❺ Adhere tiles.

## Teacher Gift Bag

Designer: Alisa Bangerter

SUPPLIES

**Cardstock:** (green, yellow, white) **Textured cardstock:** (blue, red) **Patterned paper:** (Black & White Alphabet from School collection) *Rusty Pickle* **Gift bag:** (black) *DMD, Inc.* **Accents:** (blue, green, red, yellow buttons) *Jesse James & Co.* **Fibers:** (printed ribbon) *Making Memories;* (green gingham ribbon, white string) **Font:** (CK Handprint) *Creating Keepsakes*

MAKES ONE 5½" SQUARE CARD

---

### APPETIZING IDEA

*To create the ribbon accents, fold a length of ribbon in half, thread string through the button holes and adhere over the ribbon. If you're using printed ribbon, you may need to cut the ribbon to properly display the text.*

---

### TIP A LA ALISA

*If you're using a standard-sized gift bag, remove the handles and cut the top off the bag to create a smaller bag. Then, reattach the handles and cover the bag with patterned paper.*

---

## Just Keep Swimming

Designer: Angelia Wigginton

SUPPLIES

**Textured cardstock:** (Bazzill White) *Bazzill Basics Paper* **Patterned paper:** (Pacific Tempo) *Scrapworks* **Accents:** (Ice Blue brads, fish buttons) *Making Memories* **Stickers:** (Pacific/Riviera labels) *Scrapworks* **Fibers:** (white thread) **Font:** (Couchlover) www.chank.com

MAKES ONE 5" SQUARE CARD

---

### TIP A LA ANGELIA

*"Just Keep Swimming" is a message of encouragement from Dori the fish in the movie, Finding Nemo. Send this card to someone who needs a boost.*

---

### SPICE IT UP

*Adapt the design for different occasions—use flower buttons to say "Happy Mother's Day", heart buttons to say "I'll Be Loving You", and star buttons to wish someone "Happy 4th of July".*

---

## Memories Album

Designer: Wendy Johnson

SUPPLIES

**Textured cardstock:** (Sprout) *Bazzill Basics Paper* **Patterned paper:** (Cassy, Ethan, Nick) *Heart & Home;* (Red Gingham) *Sandylion* **Album:** *Canson* **Accents:** (light green label holder, pink brads) *K&Company;* (heart acrylic charm) *Doodlebug Design* **Fibers:** (pink, red, white assorted ribbon; white thread; white string)

MAKES ONE 7" x 6" ALBUM

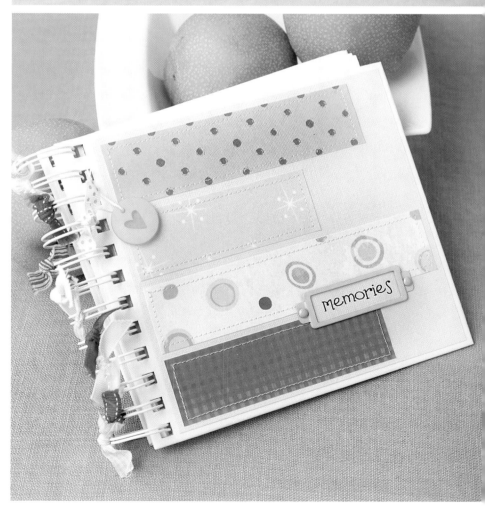

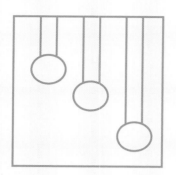

# We Thank You

Designer: Wendy Johnson

## SUPPLIES

**Cardstock:** (Soft Ivory Weathered Wood Solid from The WoodStone collection) *Cloud 9 Design* **Textured cardstock:** (Coral) *Die Cuts With a View* **Patterned paper:** (Taffy Pattern) *Carolee's Creations* **Accents:** (metal-rimmed tags) *Avery* **Stickers:** (epoxy sentiments) *Jo-Ann Stores* **Fibers:** (coral grosgrain ribbon) *Die Cuts With a View*; (white thread) **Adhesive:** foam squares

MAKES ONE 5¾" SQUARE CARD

## INSTRUCTIONS

❶ Make card from Coral cardstock. ❷ Cut square of patterned paper; mat with Soft Ivory Weathered Wood Solid and adhere. ❸ Adhere three graduated ribbon lengths to matted piece; zigzag-stitch center. ❹ Adhere matted piece to card. ❺ Affix stickers to tags; adhere.

## Cherish

Designer: Linda Beeson

SUPPLIES

**Cardstock:** (olive green, white) **Textured cardstock:** (Coral) *Bazzill Basics Paper* **Patterned paper:** (Circle Flowers from Dynamic collection) *Autumn Leaves* **Rub-ons:** (flower, circles) *Autumn Leaves*; (sentiment) *7gypsies* **Stickers:** (Small FoofaBet alphabet) *Autumn Leaves*

MAKES ONE 5½" SQUARE CARD

### SPICE IT UP

*When you look at clouds in the sky, it's fun to identify different forms that clouds become—a pig, a donut, or a car. As you look at a card sketch, use your imagination in the same way. Picture the different forms that the design can take. A row of bars and circles can become flowers, lollipops, traffic signs, yo-yos, or zoo animals.*

## Fabric Flower Trio

Designer: Sande Krieger

SUPPLIES

**Patterned paper:** (Emblem, Thrifty Dots from Thrift Store collection; Script, Tea Rose from Spring Pageantry collection) *Autumn Leaves* **Dye ink:** (Vintage Photo) *Ranger Industries* **Accents:** (canvas flowers) *Autumn Leaves*; (antique copper decorative brads) **Fibers:** (brown thread)

MAKES ONE 5" SQUARE CARD

### ADD SOME FLAVOR

*Lightly sponge the card and flowers with ink to enhance the antique look.*

## USA

Designer: Dee Gallimore-Perry

SUPPLIES

**Cardstock:** (White) *Bazzill Basics Paper* **Patterned paper:** (Outback Country, Outback Safari) *Scrappy Cat Creations*; (Canvas with Black Stars, Gold Stars) *Sweetwater* **Rubber stamps:** (Jessie's Letter alphabet) *Turtle Press* **Dye ink:** (Basic Black) *Stampin' Up!* **Accents:** (clear acrylic buttons) *7gypsies* **Fibers:** (cream thread, jute) **Other:** sandpaper

MAKES ONE 4" SQUARE CARD

### APPETIZING IDEA

*Decorate the buttons to match the card. Adhere a clear button to each patterned paper using clear liquid adhesive. When dry, trim around the edge of the buttons with a craft knife, pierce the holes, and tie with jute.*

### ADD SOME FLAVOR

*Sand the edges of the card to match the weathered marks on the patterned paper.*

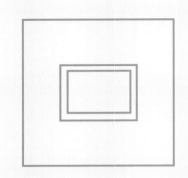

# Friendship Fold-Out

Designer: Wendy Johnson

SUPPLIES

**Cardstock:** (white) **Textured cardstock:** (Bazzill White) *Bazzill Basics Paper* **Patterned paper:** (Kiwi Splatter, Lunch Sack Splatter from The Woodmark collection, Limeade/Jalapeno from Homespun collection) *Bo-Bunny Press* **Rubber stamp:** (daisy) **Watermark ink:** *Tsukineko* **Accents:** (silver brads) *Creative Imaginations*; (light green brad) *The Happy Hammer*; (copper flower, copper flower charm) *Nunn Design*; (copper zipper pull) *All My Memories*; (D rings) **Fibers:** (green striped ribbon) *May Arts*; (tan gingham ribbon) *Creative Impressions*; (striped twill ribbon, white thread) **Font:** (Fairy Princess) *www.twopeasinabucket.com*

MAKES ONE 6" SQUARE CARD

## INSTRUCTIONS

❶ Cut Lunch Sack Splatter paper to finished size; adhere to white cardstock. Stitch edge and attach silver brads to corners. ❷ Cut 9" x 3" piece of white cardstock; score every 3" and accordion-fold to make book. ❸ Cut 3" square of Limeade/Jalapeno paper. Stamp repeatedly and stitch edges. Adhere to book cover. ❹ Print sentiment on Kiwi Splatter paper; trim and adhere inside book. Attach flower with light green brad. ❺ To make belt, sew together two lengths of twill ribbon back-to-back. Thread one end through D rings; fold end and stitch in place. Fold and stitch opposite end. ❻ Wrap belt around book; mat with Bazzill White cardstock. Adhere to card. Fasten belt and accent with ribbon and charms.

INSIDE

## Best Wishes

Designer: Michelle Tardie

**SUPPLIES**

**Patterned paper:** (Rector Street, West Thames Street from Battery Park collection) *Imagination Project* **Card:** (textured purple gatefold) *Die Cuts With a View* **Accents:** (metal-rimmed tag) *K&Company*; (light green picture hangers) *Daisy D's*; (white safety pin) *Making Memories* **Stickers:** (sentiment, dragonfly) *K&Company* **Fibers:** (yellow grosgrain ribbon) *Making Memories* **Other:** sandpaper

MAKES ONE 5½" SQUARE CARD

## Homework Helpers Gift Bag

Designer: Alice Golden

**SUPPLIES**

**Textured cardstock:** (Licorice) *Bazzill Basics Paper* **Patterned paper:** (Black & White Alphabet, Composition from School collection) *Rusty Pickle* **Cellophane bag; Accents:** (school tool charms) *Karen Foster Design*; (staples) **Stickers:** (homework, math, alphabet) *Karen Foster Design* **Fibers:** (white floss) *Karen Foster Design*; (school days ribbon) *Making Memories* **Tools:** (1⅝" square punch) *McGill*; (sanding file) *Making Memories* **Other:** treats

MAKES ONE 4½" SQUARE CARD

### TIP A LA ALICE

*Cut a 4½" x 11" strip of cardstock; score and fold. Punch a window through the bag front, and decorate it with patterned paper and stickers. Fill the cellophane bag with treats, put it in the packet, and staple in place. Punch two holes through the top of the pouch; tie it closed with ribbon.*

## Thankful for You

Designer: Wendy Sue Anderson

**SUPPLIES**

**Transparency sheet:** *Hammermill* **Accent:** (bookplate) *Creative Imaginations* **Paint:** (Buttercup) *Making Memories* **Accents:** (yellow hydrangea, black brad) *Making Memories* **Fibers:** (black, yellow polka dot ribbon) **Tools:** bone folder

MAKES ONE 4" SQUARE CARD

### TIP A LA WENDY SUE

*Use a bone folder to carefully fold the transparency—it can be difficult to fold! Accent the card edges with paint or solvent ink.*

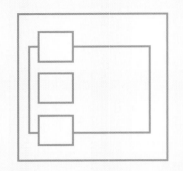

## Tokens of Congrats

Designer: Jana Millen

### SUPPLIES

**Cardstock:** (White) *Bazzill Basics Paper*
**Textured cardstock:** (Dark Tangerine, Hazard, Lily White) *Bazzill Basics Paper* **Patterned paper:** (Cathode Bungalow from Skinny collection) *Scrapworks* **Accents:** (flower acrylic charms) *Doodlebug Design* **Rub-ons:** (Classic alphabet) *KI Memories* **Fibers:** (orange gingham ribbon) *Offray*; (white thread)

MAKES ONE 5¼" SQUARE CARD

### INSTRUCTIONS

❶ Make card from White cardstock. Cover front with Hazard cardstock. ❷ Cut Dark Tangerine cardstock slightly smaller than card; stitch edges and adhere. ❸ Cut 4½"x 3" piece of patterned paper; mat with Lily White cardstock and stitch edges. Spell "Congrats" with rub-ons. Adhere to card. ❹ Mat three 1" squares of Lily White with Hazard. Tie ribbon through charms and adhere. Adhere squares to card.

## Silver Joy

Designer: Wendy Johnson

SUPPLIES
**Cardstock:** (cream, light green) **Textured cardstock:** (Pomegranate) *Bazzill Basics Paper* **Patterned paper:** (Winter Berries) *Bo-Bunny Press* **Accents:** (silver metal alphabet) *Pressed Petals* **Fibers:** (cream thread)
MAKES ONE 6" SQUARE CARD

## A Little Hello

Designer: Amber Crosby

SUPPLIES
**Cardstock:** (Light Racy Raspberry) *WorldWin* **Patterned paper:** (Pink Fusion) *Karen Foster Design* **Transparency sheet; Accents:** (wooden tag) *Chatterbox;* (flower sequins) *Doodlebug Design* **Rub-ons:** (Heidi alphabet) *Making Memories* **Fibers:** (pink gingham ribbon) *American Crafts* **Tools:** (1¼" square punch) *Family Treasures*
MAKES ONE 6" SQUARE CARD

### TIP A LA AMBER
*Adhere a piece of transparency sheet behind the card windows, and add the flower sequins. Adhere a layer of cardstock inside the card to keep the sequins in place and provide a clean, finished look.*

## Spooky Greetings

Designer: Alisa Bangerter

SUPPLIES
**Cardstock:** (white) **Textured cardstock:** (Fawn) *Bazzill Basics Paper* **Patterned paper:** (My Family Stripe/Blue) *My Mind's Eye;* (Black on Worn Text) *Scenic Route Paper Co.* **Walnut ink:** *Fiber Scraps* **Paper accents:** (black photo corners) *Avery* **Accents:** (pumpkin wire brads) *Karen Foster Design;* (natural fabric swatches) *Junkitz* **Fibers:** (natural twill ribbon) *Wrights;* (black gingham ribbon) *Jo-Ann Stores;* (orange gingham ribbon) *Offray* **Font:** (CK Opa's Hand) *Creating Keepsakes* **Software:** (Word) *Microsoft* **Adhesive:** foam tape **Other:** sandpaper
MAKES ONE 5½" SQUARE CARD

### TIP A LA ALISA
*Add a spooky look to the card accents: crumple and/or sand the paper pieces and apply walnut ink to the ribbon.*

### APPETIZING IDEA

*To print colored text pieces, follow these steps.*

*1 Open a new document in Microsoft Word. Note: Be sure the Drawing Toolbar is displayed.*

*2 Select the text box icon on the Drawing Toolbar. Size the box and type the text as desired.*

*3 To change the font color, highlight the text and select the A icon on the Formatting Toolbar. In the drop-down box, select the desired color.*

*4 To change the background color, select Format > Text Box on the Toolbar. Click the "Colors and Lines" tab. In the Fill Color drop-down box, select the desired color.*

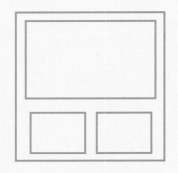

## For a Sweet Friend

Designer: Wendy Johnson

### SUPPLIES

**Cardstock:** (cream) **Patterned paper:** (A Charmed Life Paisley/Red, Mom & Me Polka Dot/Tan, Pretty Little Girl Stripe/Pink) *My Mind's Eye* **Paper accents:** (sentiments) *My Mind's Eye* **Accents:** (large silver brads) *Creative Imaginations*; (small silver brads) *Making Memories* **Fibers:** (white thread) **Tools:** (daisy punch) *EK Success* **Other:** sandpaper

MAKES ONE 6" SQUARE CARD

### INSTRUCTIONS

❶ Make card from cream cardstock. Cover front with Tan paper. ❷ Cut 5½" x 4" piece of Mom & Me Polka Dot paper; stitch edges. ❸ Punch flowers from Pink, Red, and Tan paper; sand edges and attach to stitched piece with large brads. Adhere to card. ❹ Trim and stitch edges of paper accents. Attach small brads and adhere to card.

## Journey

Designer: Sande Krieger

SUPPLIES

**Cardstock:** (black) **Patterned paper:** (Da Vinci Tiles) *Design Originals*; (Stucco from Motifica collection) *BasicGrey* **Accents:** (chipboard tiles) *Bazzill Basics Paper*; (metal-rimmed tag) *Office Depot*; (jump ring) *Making Memories* **Rub-ons:** (alphabet) *Making Memories* **Stickers:** (rulers) *EK Success*; (alphabet) *Me & My Big Ideas*; (alphabet, round tag) *7gypsies* **Fibers:** (black satin ribbon) *Offray*

MAKES ONE 5½" SQUARE CARD

## Halloween Wishes

Designer: Michelle Tardie

SUPPLIES

**Textured cardstock:** (Dark Black, Honeycomb) *Bazzill Basics Paper* **Patterned paper:** (Spooky Stripes from Halloween collection) *Creative Imaginations* **Accents:** (black brads) *American Crafts* **Stickers:** (Halloween set) *Creative Imaginations* **Adhesive:** foam squares

MAKES ONE 5" SQUARE CARD

### TIP A LA MICHELLE

*To give the flat stickers dimension, mat them with Honeycomb cardstock, add brads, and adhere them to the card with foam squares.*

## Happy Thanksgiving

Designer: Susan Neal

SUPPLIES

**Cardstock:** (Natural) *Bazzill Basics Paper* **Textured cardstock:** (Flowerpot, Pinecone) *Bazzill Basics Paper* **Patterned paper:** (Thanksgiving from Holidays & Seasons pack) *Hot Off The Press* **Rubber stamps:** (Happy Thanksgiving) *Delta*; (Wheat Block) *Magenta* **Pigment ink:** (Roussillon) *Clearsnap*; (Vintage Sepia) *Tsukineko* **Accent:** (sprig of wheat or other grain) **Fibers:** (natural craft thread) **Adhesive:** foam tape

MAKES ONE 5" SQUARE CARD

### TIP A LA SUSAN

*Tie the sprig of wheat or other grain with thread and staple it to the card front. Secure wayward grains in place with adhesive dots.*

### SPICE IT UP

*Adjust the elements of the card sketch to fit the size of the stamped images and other accents you want to use.*

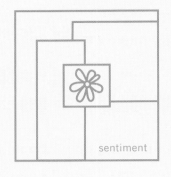

## Get Well Soon

Designer: Heather D. White

### SUPPLIES

**Patterned paper:** (Blue, Dots, Stripes from Grandpa's Closet collection) *Fancy Pants Designs* **Dye ink:** (Van Dyke Brown) *Ranger Industries* **Sticker:** (daisy) *Fancy Pants Designs* **Fonts:** (SP Purkage) *www.scrapsupply.com*; (Century Gothic) *www.fonts.com*

MAKES ONE 4½" SQUARE CARD

### INSTRUCTIONS

**1** Make card from Stripes paper. **2** Print sentiment on Blue paper; trim to fit card front, ink edges, and adhere. **3** Cut 3¼" x 2" piece of Dots paper, and 1¼" x 4" piece of Stripes paper; ink edges and adhere. **4** Add sticker.

## Enjoy the Journey

Designer: Ann Powell

SUPPLIES

**Cardstock:** (cream, light green) **Paper:** (Green/Alpine Tempo, Alpine Delay/Light Green) *Scrapworks* **Rub-on:** (sentiment) *Making Memories* **Stickers:** (color blocks) *Scrapworks* **Other:** sandpaper

MAKES ONE 3" SQUARE CARD

**TIP A LA ANN**

*The stickers provide a sharp, clean contrast to the sanded paper on the card. Enjoy arranging abstract stickers on your card—they're appropriate for any occasion!*

## A Flower for Mom

Designer: Michelle Tardie

SUPPLIES

**Textured cardstock:** (Nautical Blue Dark) *Prism* **Patterned paper:** (Blue/Sunshine Daisies, Yellow/Sunshine Stripes) *We R Memory Keepers* **Accents:** (brushed copper, silver brads) *Impress Rubber Stamps*; (yellow daisy) *Making Memories* **Rub-ons:** (alphabet) *Creative Imaginations* **Fibers:** (twine) **Other:** sandpaper

MAKES ONE 4" SQUARE CARD

## Buddies Wall Hanging

Designer: Wendy Johnson

SUPPLIES

**Textured cardstock:** (Hazard) *Bazzill Basics Paper* **Patterned paper:** (Dorm Diamonds, Dorm Plaid) *Chatterbox* **Photo; Frame:** (white) *Target* **Accents:** (blue, orange acrylic heart buttons) *Junkitz*; (Sunsoaked alphabet tag, Celery alphabet tile) *Making Memories*; (cream fabric alphabet brad) *Jo-Ann Stores*; (blue wood alphabet) *Westrim Crafts*; (chipboard alphabet) *Li'l Davis Designs*; (alphabet brad) *Colorbok*; (twill tag alphabet) *Carolee's Creations*; (staple) **Fibers:** (striped grosgrain ribbon) *Making Memories*; (white thread)

MAKES ONE 9" SQUARE WALL HANGING

**SECRET INGREDIENTS**

*If you're using brightly-colored paper and accents, use a black and white photo so the colors won't compete. When using a colored photo, use accents in neutral tones.*

# CHAPTER 4

# Made in Minutes

Cook up cards in no time with these simple recipes.

The small 3" x 3½" size is perfect to attach to gifts

but still brimming with flavor.

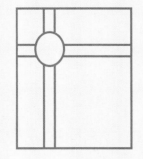

# Oh Baby

Designer: Heather D. White

### SUPPLIES

**Cardstock:** (white) **Textured cardstock:** (light blue) **Patterned paper:** (Pastel Blue on Yellow) Perky Plaids, *Keeping Memories Alive* **Accent:** (diaper) Jolee's By You, *EK Success* **Stickers:** (Time Saver Alpha Blocks) *All My Memories* **Fibers:** (yellow rickrack) **Tools:** scissors, ⅜" square punch

### INSTRUCTIONS

❶ Make card from white cardstock. Cut Pastel Blue on Yellow paper to fit card; adhere. ❷ Adhere rickrack and diaper to card. ❸ Mat alphabet stickers with light blue cardstock and adhere to card to spell "baby."

135

## Adventure Waiting to Happen

Designer: Marla Bird

SUPPLIES

**Cardstock:** (Cream) *Provo Craft* **Patterned paper:** (Burlap) *The Paper Loft* **Paper accent:** (boat stamp) Transport Stamps, *Provo Craft* **Rub-ons:** (Postage Cancellation) Impress-on, *Creative Imaginations*; (adventure from Journey) Simply Stated Mini, *Making Memories* **Accent:** (black elastic cord) *7gypsies* **Tools:** scissors

## Happy Birthday to You

Designer: Sande Krieger

SUPPLIES

**Textured cardstock:** (Pumpkin) *Bazzill Basics Paper* **Patterned paper:** (Birthday Word Find from Birthday set) Collection II, *KI Memories* **Sticker:** (Happy Birthday epoxy) Pocket Pebbles, Jone Hallmark, *Creative Imaginations* **Tools:** scissors

## Hi There

Designer: Kathleen Paneitz

SUPPLIES

**Cardstock:** (white) **Textured cardstock:** (Baby Pink) *Bazzill Basics Paper* **Patterned paper:** (Citrus Stripe) *KI Memories* **Accent:** (hi there from Friendship 1) Woven Labels, *Making Memories* **Tools:** scissors, sewing machine **Other:** pink thread

**SPICE IT UP**

*Rotate the design to create a tent-fold card.*

## Tree Token

Designer: Wendy Sue Anderson

SUPPLIES

**Textured cardstock:** (Ivy) Bazzill Basics Paper
**Patterned paper:** (Scarlet Dots) Rec
Room Collection, (Cabin Stripe) Cabin
Collection, *Chatterbox* **Dye ink:** (Sand) Memories,
*Stewart Superior Corp.* **Accent:** (tree Token)
Christmas, *Doodlebug Design* **Fibers:** (Antique
gingham ribbon) *Making Memories* **Adhesive:**
(dots) *Glue Dots International;*
double-sided tape **Tools:** scissors

## The Magic of Christmas

Designer: Dee Gallimore-Perry

SUPPLIES

**Cardstock:** (dark blue) **Rub-ons:** (BELIEVE, the
magic of Christmas from Christmas 2) Simply
Stated Mini, *Making Memories* **Accent:**
(Snowflake) Jolee's by You, *EK Success* **Fibers:**
(silver ribbon) *Nicole Industries* **Adhesive:** (mini
dots) *Glue Dots International* **Tools:** scissors,
craft knife

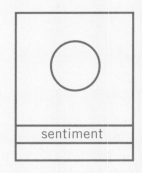

sentiment

## Love Bug

Designer: Heather D. White

### SUPPLIES

**Cardstock:** (black) **Patterned paper:** (Fuchsia Twine Plaid) Watercolor Collection, *Making Memories* **Shrink plastic:** (Black) *Stampin' Up!* **Accents:** (metal-rimmed vellum tag) *Making Memories*; (pink bug button) *Blumenthal Lansing*; (black label tape) *Dymo* **Fibers:** (black and white ribbon) *Making Memories* **Adhesive:** (dots) *Glue Dots International*; glue stick **Tools:** (Heart die cut, die-cut machine) Sizzix, *Provo Craft/Ellison*; (label) *Dymo*; scissors, heat tool or baking sheet and oven

### INSTRUCTIONS

❶ Make card from cardstock. Cut patterned paper slightly smaller than card; adhere. ❷ Die-cut heart from shrink plastic; shrink with heat tool or oven, following manufacturer's instructions. ❸ Tie ribbon through top of tag and adhere to card. Adhere bug and heart to card. ❹ Create "LOVE BUG" label and adhere to bottom of card.

# Boo!

Designer: Marla Bird

SUPPLIES

*All supplies from Pebbles Inc. unless otherwise noted.*

**Patterned paper:** (Halloween Word/Stripe) ETC **Stickers:** (Labels alphabet) Real Life **Accent:** (ghost Shaker Bubble) I Kan Dee **Adhesive:** no source **Tools:** (scissors) no source

# Admire

Designer: Marla Bird

SUPPLIES

**Patterned cardstock:** (Riley double-sided) *American Crafts* **Accent:** (Admire bottle cap) *Li'l Davis Designs* **Rub-on:** (Love from Baby) Simply Stated Mini, *Making Memories* **Fasteners:** (silver brads) *Pebbles Inc.* **Adhesive:** double-sided tape, foam tape **Tools:** scissors

# Hey, Thanks!

Designer: Wendy Sue Anderson

SUPPLIES

*All supplies from Making Memories unless otherwise noted.*

**Patterned cardstock:** (Handbag Stripe, Stiletto Stripe, Uptown Dot) Cosmopolitan Collection **Paper accents:** (Variety Bead Moulding Strip) **Accent:** (hey, thanks! from Thanks 1 set) Woven Labels **Fastener:** (silver brad) **Adhesive:** no source **Tools:** (scissors) no source

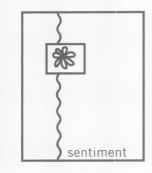

sentiment

## I Love You

Designer: Heather D. White

### SUPPLIES

Cardstock: (white)

Patterned paper: (Botanicals, Pink Argyle) *Rusty Pickle* **Accent:** (heart) Charmed Plaques, *Making Memories* **Rub-on:** (I love you) PSX, *Duncan* **Adhesive:** metal, glue stick **Tools:** scissors

### INSTRUCTIONS

❶ Make card from white cardstock. ❷ Cut Botanicals paper to fit left side of card; adhere. Cut Pink Argyle paper to fit card front; tear left edge and adhere. ❸ Adhere heart plaque with metal adhesive. ❹ Apply rub-on.

## Hi

Designer: Sande Krieger

SUPPLIES

**Textured cardstock:** (peach) **Patterned paper:** (Powder Blossoms) Powder Room Collection, *Chatterbox* **Accents:** (hi epoxy rectangle) Ice Candy, Icicles, *KI Memories*; (red flower) **Fastener:** (silver nail) Lost Art Treasures, *American Label & Tag* **Tools:** scissors, eyelet-setting tools

## We've Moved

Designer: Michelle Tardie

SUPPLIES

**Textured cardstock:** (Papaya) *Bazzill Basics Paper* **Patterned paper:** (Green Tea Flower from Camouflage set, Lemonade Linen from Surf set) Collection II, *KI Memories* **Accent:** (home button) *Sue Dreamer* **Font:** (CK Journaling) "The Best of Creative Lettering Combo" CD, *Creating Keepsakes* **Adhesive:** (dots) *Glue Dots International* **Tools:** scissors, computer and printer

## Thinking of You on Easter

Designer: Nichole Heady

SUPPLIES

*All supplies from Stampin' Up! unless otherwise noted.*

**Cardstock:** (Blush Blossom, Ultrasmooth White) **Vellum:** (floral) *The Paper Patch* **Rubber stamps:** (egg from Year Round Fun II set, happy from Everyday Flexible Phrases set, I'm Here set) **Watermark ink:** VersaMark, *Tsukineko* **Embossing powder:** (White Detail) **Dimensional glaze:** (Crystal Effects) **Accents:** (white seed beads) **Adhesive:** (mini dots) *Glue Dots International*; (vellum adhesive) no source **Tools:** (¼" hole punch) *Fiskars*; (scissors, heat tool, tweezers, toothpick) no source

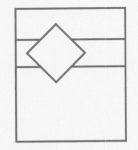

## Have Fun

Designer: Heather D. White

### SUPPLIES

**Cardstock:** (Gable Green) *Stampin' Up!* **Patterned paper:** (Blue Bikini) Coastline Collection, *Making Memories* **Accent:** (sunglasses button) *Buttons Galore & More* **Rub-on:** (have fun from Expressions) Simply Stated Mini, *Making Memories* **Fibers:** (blue with green dots ribbon) *May Arts* **Adhesive:** dots, glue stick **Tools:** scissors

### INSTRUCTIONS

❶ Make card from cardstock. ❷ Cut patterned paper slightly smaller than card; adhere. ❸ Adhere ribbon across top of card. Adhere sunglasses with dots. ❹ Apply rub-on sentiment.

## Black & White

Designer: Sande Krieger

SUPPLIES
**Cardstock:** (white) **Rubber stamp:** (Old French Writing) *Hero Arts* **Solvent ink:** (Jet Black) StāzOn, *Tsukineko* **Accent:** (clear acrylic buckle) *Jo-Ann Stores* **Fibers:** (black and white striped ribbon) *May Arts*; (black grosgrain ribbon) *Offray* **Tools:** scissors

## Shimmering Tile

Designer: Kathleen Paneitz

SUPPLIES
**Cardstock:** (white) **Patterned paper:** (Pink Petite Pinstripes) *Paperfever* **Accent:** (Pink Flower Embossed Square) *ScrapYard 329* **Fasteners:** (white flower eyelet) *Creative Impressions*; (purple brad) *Magic Scraps* **Fibers:** (Celery grosgrain ribbon) *Making Memories* **Tools:** scissors, eyelet-setting tools

## Little Leaf

Designer: Michelle Tardie

SUPPLIES
**Textured cardstock:** (Dark Fawn) *Bazzill Basics Paper* **Paper accents:** (leaf) The Great Outdoors Sampler, (border) Camping Border Sampler, *O'Scrap!* **Adhesive:** (double-sided tape) Scotch, *3M* **Tools:** scissors

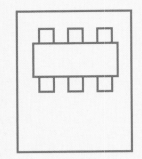

# Make a Wish

Designer: Heather D. White

### SUPPLIES

**Cardstock:** (orange, white) **Patterned paper:** (Terra-Cotta Funky Swirls) Watercolor Collection, *Making Memories* **Accent:** (birthday candles) **Fibers:** (orange gingham ribbon) *Offray*; (white floss) *DMC* **Font:** (Blueberry Pie) *www.two peasinabucket.com* **Dimensional glaze:** Crystal Effects, *Stampin' Up!* **Tools:** scissors, computer and printer, ⅛" hole punch, sewing machine **Other:** white thread

## INSTRUCTIONS

❶ Make card from white cardstock. Cut Terra-Cotta Funky Swirls paper to fit card front; adhere. ❷ Machine-stitch edges of card. ❸ Tie ribbon around candles and adhere to card with dimensional glaze. ❹ Print "make a wish" on white cardstock; trim into tag and mat with orange cardstock. Punch hole through top and tie to ribbon with floss.

## Congrats!

Designer: Michelle Tardie

SUPPLIES

**Textured cardstock:** (Blue Bonnet, Dark Olive, Rosey, Sherbet) *Bazzill Basics Paper* **Pigment ink:** (Black) ColorBox, *Clearsnap* **Accent:** (Congrats metal tag) *Gartner Studios* **Sticker:** (polka-dot tag) Spring Tag Alongs, *Deluxe Designs* **Fastener:** (Scarlet Rivet) *Chatterbox* **Fibers:** (burgundy, yellow) **Adhesive:** (double-sided tape) Scotch, *3M* **Tools:** scissors **Other:** baby powder, hole punch

**APPETIZING IDEA**

*To create the tag embellishment, apply baby powder to the back of the tag sticker to remove the stickiness and make it easier to handle. Attach the rivet to the tag sticker and tie the metal tag through the rivet with fibers.*

## Miss Ewe

Designer: Marla Bird

SUPPLIES

**Cardstock:** (Woodchip) *Pebbles Inc.* **Patterned paper:** (Country Sheep) *The Paper Lady* **Accent:** (clear acrylic label) *Stampabilities* **Stickers:** (Large Vowel alphabet) Alphabitties, *Provo Craft* **Fibers:** (raffia) **Tools:** hole punch, scissors, pencil

## Old-Fashioned Birthday

Designer: Sande Krieger

SUPPLIES

**Textured cardstock:** (Blue) **Accent:** (happy birthday from Birthday 2 set) Woven Labels, *Making Memories* **Fasteners:** (Forget-Me-Not Blue brads) *Lasting Impressions for Paper* **Fibers:** (black gingham ribbon) *May Arts* **Tools:** scissors

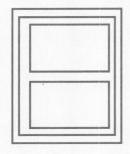

## Hugs & Kisses

Designer: Heather D. White

### SUPPLIES

**Cardstock:** (olive, yellow) **Patterned paper:** (Tile) Simple Expressions, *Keeping Memories Alive* **Color medium:** (brown chalk) *Craft-T Products* **Paper accent:** (Walnut ink tag) *Rusty Pickle* **Accents:** (hugs, kisses twill labels) Love Forever, *All My Memories*; (antique gold spiral clip) *Making Memories* **Fastener:** (Gold Heart eyelet) *Woohoo Wowies* **Tools:** scissors, chalk applicator, eyelet-setting tools, ruler

### INSTRUCTIONS

❶ Make card from olive cardstock. Cut Tile paper slightly smaller than card; adhere. ❷ Cut two 2½" x 1¼" pieces from tag. Cut two pieces of yellow cardstock slightly smaller than tag pieces; randomly tear, curl, and chalk edges. Adhere to tag pieces. ❸ Chalk edges of labels and adhere. ❹ Add clip and brad; adhere pieces to card.

## Thoughts from Afar

Designer: Sande Krieger

SUPPLIES
**Cardstock:** (olive) **Patterned paper:** (script) *DMD, Inc.* **Dye ink:** (Vintage Photo) Distress Ink, *Ranger Industries* **Paper accent:** (white cardstock tag) *Making Memories* **Stickers:** (postage stamps) Nostalgiques, *EK Success* **Fibers:** (linen string) **Font:** (Book Antiqua) *Microsoft* **Adhesive:** glue stick, repositionable **Tools:** scissors, paper-piercing tool, computer and printer

### APPETIZING IDEAS

*To print "Miss You" on the small tag, first print the text on a sheet of paper. Then, adhere the tag over the text with repositionable adhesive. Run the paper through the printer again.*

## Butterfly Stamps

Designer: Michelle Tardie

SUPPLIES
**Textured cardstock:** (Red Robin) *Bazzill Basics Paper* **Patterned paper:** (Gingham Dot Garnet, Script Garnet) Gingham Rose Collection, *Daisy D's* **Stickers:** (Butterfly Stamps) *Provo Craft* **Fasteners:** (red brads) *Making Memories* **Adhesive:** (double-sided tape) Scotch, *3M* **Tools:** scissors

### TIPS A LA MICHELLE

*Pierce a hole through the cardstock or paper to make brad insertion easier.*

*Make it easier to design your cards by using patterned paper from the same product line.*

## Feel Better

Designer: Nichole Heady

SUPPLIES
**Cardstock:** (Baroque Burgundy) *Stampin' Up!* **Patterned paper:** (Quadrant Canopie) *7gypsies* **Specialty paper:** (burgundy embossed) **Stickers:** (Chocolate Brown Leather alphabet) Century, *All My Memories*; (green alphabet) **Fastener:** (antique brass square brad) *All My Memories* **Tools:** (Daisy punch) *Stampin' Up!*; scissors

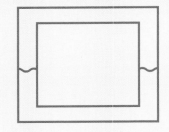

# Birthday Wish

Designer: Heather D. White

### SUPPLIES

**Cardstock:** (white) **Textured cardstock:** (Baby Pink, Limeade, Rosebud) *Bazzill Basics Paper* **Accents:** (yellow slide mount) *Boxer Scrapbook Productions*; (yellow buttons) Dress It Up, *Jesse James & Co.*; (alphabet beads) *Darice* **Fibers:** (lavender gingham ribbon) *Offray*; (white floss) *DMC* **Adhesive:** (dots) *Glue Dots International*; glue stick **Tools:** scissors, sewing machine, needle **Other:** white thread

## INSTRUCTIONS

❶ Make card from Baby Pink cardstock. Cut white cardstock slightly smaller than card; adhere. Machine-stitch edges. ❷ Adhere ribbon to center of card, wrapping ends behind front flap. ❸ Cut white cardstock to fit behind slide mount. Cut one candle each from Baby Pink, Limeade, and Rosebud cardstock; adhere to white piece. Stitch buttons above candles with floss. Adhere candle piece behind slide mount. ❹ Spell "WISH" with alphabet beads on slide mount using adhesive dots.

## Bumble Bee Greetings

Designer: Wendy Sue Anderson

SUPPLIES
**Cardstock:** (yellow) **Textured cardstock:** (blue)
**Dye ink:** (Sand) Memories, *Stewart Superior Corp.*
**Paper accent:** (bee tag) Embossible Designs, *We R Memory Keepers* **Fibers:** (white organdy ribbon) *Offray* **Adhesive:** (foam squares) *Making Memories*; (glue stick) **Tools:** scissors

## Boy Oh Boy

Designer: Ann Powell

SUPPLIES
**Textured cardstock:** (light blue, bluish green)
**Patterned paper:** (Pool Party) *Stampin' Up!* **Rub-on:** (BOY OH BOY) Beatnik Boys, *SEI* **Fasteners:** (dark, light, medium blue brads) *The Happy Hammer* **Adhesive:** foam tape, glue stick
**Tools:** scissors

## Heaven Sent

Designer: Sande Krieger

SUPPLIES
**Textured cardstock:** (Baby Pink) *Bazzill Basics Paper* **Patterned paper:** (Pink Letter, Pink Paisley) *Rusty Pickle* **Dye ink:** (Vintage Photo) Distress Ink, *Ranger Industries* **Rub-ons:** (heaven sent from Baby) Simply Stated Mini, *Making Memories* **Fibers:** (brown polka-dot ribbon) *The Weathered Door* **Adhesive:** dots, glue stick **Tools:** scissors, sewing machine **Other:** baby photo, sandpaper, brown thread

### APPETIZING IDEA
*Cut two pieces of Pink Letter paper to fit card;
cut in half. Adhere each piece next to fold
on each side of card. Zigzag-stitch along outside
edge of each Pink Letter piece.*

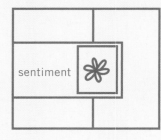

sentiment

## Happy Birthday

Designer: Heather D. White

### SUPPLIES

**Cardstock:** (cream) **Patterned paper:** (Billiard Stripes/Blue Weave) Billiard Room Collection, (Great Plaid/Brown Weave) Great Room Collection, (Sun Room Stripe) Sun Room Collection, *Chatterbox* **Color medium:** (brown chalk) *Craf-T Products* **Paper accent:** (Happy Birthday word strips) *Making Memories* **Accent:** (rusty tin star) *DCC Crafts* **Fastener:** (antique gold brad) *Making Memories* **Tools:** scissors **Other:** sandpaper

### INSTRUCTIONS

❶ Make card from cardstock. Trim Blue Weave and Brown Weave paper to fit each half of card; adhere. ❷ Cut piece of Sun Room Stripe paper; sand and adhere to card. ❸ Sand card edges. ❹ Adhere star and word strips. Add brad.

### For Baby

Designer: Wendy Sue Anderson

SUPPLIES

*All supplies from Doodlebug Design unless otherwise noted.*

**Cardstock:** (Bubble Blue, Limeade); (white) no source **Patterned paper:** (Baby Talk Boy) **Sticker:** (turtle) Baby Boy **Rub-ons:** (Limeade Large alphabet) **Adhesive:** (foam squares) *Making Memories* **Tools:** (scissors) no source **Other:** (baby powder) no source

### Just Wanted to Say Hi

Designer: Lori Allred

SUPPLIES

**Cardstock:** (Caution Solid from Lava Lamp set) Collection III, *KI Memories* **Patterned paper:** (Hot Pink Mini Bangles, Lava Lamp Rhinestone from Lava Lamp set) Collection III, *KI Memories* **Paper accent:** (flower square) Funky Frames & Labels, Lava Lamp, *KI Memories* **Rub-ons:** (Rummage alphabet) Simply Stated Alphabets, *Making Memories* **Adhesive:** foam tape, glue stick **Tools:** scissors

### Have a Great Day

Designer: Dee Gallimore-Perry

SUPPLIES

**Cardstock:** (Cotton Candy Solid from Eye Candy set) Collection III, *KI Memories* **Patterned paper:** (Lemonade Capri Stripe, Sunrise Capri Stripe) Collection I, *KI Memories* **Paper accent:** (gift die cut) Happy Birthday, *Me & My Big Ideas*; (white cardstock tag) *Making Memories* **Accent:** (metal-rimmed vellum tag) *Making Memories* **Stickers:** (Large Vowel alphabet) Half-A-Bitties, *Provo Craft* **Fibers:** (orange, pink, yellow craft thread) *DMC* **Tools:** scissors

# Stars 'n Hearts

Designer: Heather D. White

SUPPLIES

**Cardstock:** (cream) **Patterned paper:** (Cinnamon Rustic Gingham) Rustic Royals, *The Paper Patch* **Accents:** (heart, star buttons) Dress It Up, *Jesse James & Co.* **Fibers:** (Navy ribbon) *Making Memories*; (cream floss) *DMC*; (twill ribbon) **Adhesive:** (adhesive machine) Sticker Maker 150, *Xyron*; (glue stick) **Tools:** scissors, needle, ruler

INSTRUCTIONS

❶ Make card from cream cardstock. Trim Cinnamon Rustic Gingham paper ¾" shorter than card and adhere.
❷ Stitch buttons along bottom with floss.
❸ Adhere Navy ribbon along center of twill ribbon, using adhesive machine; tie around front flap of card.

## Pretty in Pewter

Designer: Sande Krieger

SUPPLIES

**Cardstock:** (blue) **Specialty paper:** (Denim Beaded Vine embossed) Artistic Scrapper, *Creative Imaginations* **Fasteners:** (pewter decorative brads) *Making Memories* **Tools:** scissors

### TIP A LA SANDE

*Adhere the Denim Beaded Vine paper to cardstock for reinforcement before making the card.*

## Blooming Love

Designer: Michelle Tardie

SUPPLIES

**Cardstock:** (White) *Bazzill Basics Paper* **Paper accents:** (Camping Border Sampler) *O'Scrap!* **Sticker:** (love) Wonderful Words, Déjà Views, *C-Thru Ruler Co.* **Fasteners:** (flower brads) Watercolor Brites, *Making Memories* **Adhesive:** (dots) *Glue Dots International* **Tools:** scissors

### TIP A LA MICHELLE

*To make the brad accents, attach the brads to matching squares from the Camping Border sampler, then cut the squares and adhere them to the card with adhesive dots.*

## Love Is All Around You

Designer: Sande Krieger

SUPPLIES

**Cardstock:** (kraft) **Patterned paper:** (gold script) Earthtones, *American Traditional Designs* **Rub-ons:** (patterned squares) Bits of Time, *American Traditional Designs* **Tools:** scissors

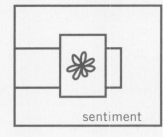

## Happy Easter

Designer: Heather D. White

### SUPPLIES

**Textured cardstock:** (Baby Pink) *Bazzill Basics Paper*
**Patterned paper:** (Lemon Simple Sponge) Watercolor Collection, *Making Memories* **Paper accent:** (button flower) Paper Bliss, *Westrim Crafts* **Fibers:** (light green grosgrain ribbon) *May Arts* **Font:** (Sitcom) *www.two peasinabucket.com* **Tools:** scissors, computer and printer

### INSTRUCTIONS

❶ Make card from cardstock. ❷ Print "happy easter" on Lemon Simple Sponge paper. Trim slightly smaller than card; adhere. ❸ Adhere ribbon to left side of card, adhering end in back. ❹ Adhere flower.

## Friends

Designer: Michelle Tardie

SUPPLIES
**Textured cardstock:** (Papaya) *Bazzill Basics Paper*
**Paper accents:** (flower, border) The Great
Outdoors Sampler, *O'Scrap!* **Sticker:** (friends)
Inspirational Words, *Tumblebeasts* **Fastener:**
(Tangerine Rivet) *Chatterbox* **Adhesive:** (double-
sided tape) Scotch, *3M* **Tools:** scissors

---

**ADD SOME FLAVOR**
*Add a little dimension to flat accents
by attaching brads or eyelets.*

---

## Butterfly Kisses & Mother's Day Wishes

Designer: Kathleen Paneitz

SUPPLIES
**Cardstock:** (white) **Patterned paper:** (Floral Linen)
Sonnets, *Creative Imaginations* **Dye ink:** (Soft
Leaf) Memories, *Stewart Superior Corp.* **Pigment
ink:** (Blue Smoke) VersaColor, *Tsukineko* **Paper
accent:** (butterfly) *K&Company* **Accents:** (blue sta-
ples) *Making Memories* **Stickers:** (Estate Sale
Moss alphabet) Sonnets, *Creative Imaginations*
**Tools:** scissors, stapler

## Thank You

Designer: Sande Krieger

SUPPLIES
**Cardstock:** (Dark Black) *Bazzill Basics Paper*
**Textured cardstock:** (Vintage) *Bazzill
Basics Paper* **Patterned paper:** (Blue Plaster)
Nostalgiques, *EK Success* **Rubber stamp:**
(thank you) *Savvy Stamps* **Pigment ink:**
(Black) ColorBox, *Clearsnap* **Accent:** (button)
Nostalgiques, *EK Success* **Fibers:** (black
gingham ribbon) *Offray* **Tools:** scissors

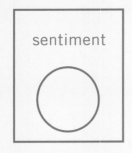

## Escape

Designer: Michelle Tardie

**SUPPLIES**
**Textured cardstock:** (Candle Glow Dark, Papaya Puree Dark) *Prism* **Accents:** (linen mesh) *Magic Mesh* **Rub-on:** (sentiment) *Making Memories* **Stickers:** (vacation) *Making Memories*; (compass) *We R Memory Keepers* **Fibers:** (twine)

INSTRUCTIONS
❶ Make card from Papaya Puree Dark cardstock. ❷ Trim Candle Glow Dark cardstock slightly smaller than card; adhere. ❸ Trim rectangle of mesh; adhere to card. ❹ Apply rub-on; adhere vacation sticker. ❺ Adhere compass sticker. ❻ Punch two holes on card. Thread twine through holes; knot.

# Happy New Year

Designer: Wendy Johnson

SUPPLIES

**Cardstock:** (Silk Scarf Blue from Cosmopolitan collection) *Making Memories*; (cream) **Patterned paper:** (Uptown Dot Blue from Cosmopolitan collection) *Making Memories* **Accent:** (epoxy sentiment) *Jo-Ann Stores* **Font:** (Rock Star) www.twopeasinabucket.com

# All About Today

Designer: Susan Neal

SUPPLIES

**Cardstock:** (White) *Bazzill Basics Paper* **Textured cardstock:** (Marigold, Papaya) *Bazzill Basics Paper* **Rubber stamp:** (sentiment) **Dye ink:** (Tea Dye) *Ranger Industries* **Pigment ink:** (Onyx Black) *Tsukineko* **Color medium:** (black pen) **Adhesive:** (½" foam squares) *Therm O Web* **Dies:** (circles) *Provo Craft/Ellison*

### TIP A LA SUSAN

*To get a perfect fit for the sun rays, lightly adhere cardstock same side up with repositionable tape. Once separated and assembled, the rays will fit together.*

# Sweets to Eat Gift Bag and Card

Designer: Dee Gallimore-Perry

SUPPLIES

**Gift bag:** (black) **Cardstock:** (Black) *Bazzill Basics Paper* **Patterned paper:** (Polka Dots from Halloween collection) *Creative Imaginations* **Accents:** (white safety pin, silver jump ring) *Making Memories* **Sticker:** (pumpkin epoxy, Halloween stickers) *Creative Imaginations* **Fibers:** (orange polka dot, green polka dot, black gingham ribbon) *Offray*; (orange thread)

MAKES ONE 8¾" x 5½" BAG

### APPETIZING IDEAS

*To quickly turn a sticker into a fun accent, apply talcum powder to the sticky side, punch a hole, and add a jump ring.*

### SECRET INGREDIENTS

*Create matching ensembles of gift bags, cards, or tags using the same recipe. It saves time and looks great, too!*

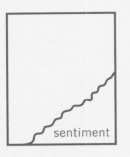

sentiment

## Foot Note

Designer: Nichole Heady

### SUPPLIES

*All supplies from Stampin' Up! unless otherwise noted.*

**Cardstock:** (Whisper White, Certainly Celery) **Rubber stamps:** (shoes, foot note from Fashion Statements set) **Dye ink:** (Classic Black, Certainly Celery, Bashful Blue) **Accents:** (glitter) **Fibers:** (white thread) no source

### INSTRUCTIONS

**1** Make card from Whisper White cardstock. **2** Stamp shoes on card with Classic Black; tint image with Certainly Celery and Bashful Blue. **3** Apply adhesive to image; add glitter. **4** Tear corner from Certainly Celery cardstock; stitch to card. **5** Stamp foot note with Classic Black on card.

## Copper Heart Anniversary

Designer: Angelia Wigginton

SUPPLIES

**Cardstock:** (natural) **Patterned paper:** (Love, Swept Away from Romantic Notions collection) *Autumn Leaves* **Accent:** (copper heart) *Pressed Petals* **Fibers:** (black stitched ribbon) *May Arts*

## Thanks Gift Bag

Designer: Wendy Johnson

SUPPLIES

**Gift bag; Cardstock:** (red) **Patterned paper:** (Multi Stripes from Bedtime Bears collection) *Zim's* **Accents:** (sentiment craft sticks) *Everlasting Keepsakes;* (flower buttons) *Jesse James & Co.* **Fibers:** (mustard striped ribbon) *May Arts;* (green gingham ribbon) *Creative Imaginations;* (red ribbon) *Li'l Davis Designs*

MAKES ONE 5¼" x 4" BAG

## Christmas Party Invitation

Designer: Sara Horton

SUPPLIES

**Cardstock:** (white, red) **Specialty paper:** (Matte photo) *Epson* **Font:** (Magic Forest) www.twopeasinabucket.com **Photo**

**APPETIZING IDEAS**

*Adding family photos or other sentimental accents makes the card personalized and meaningful.*

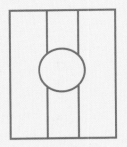

## Make a Wish

Designer: Wendy Johnson

SUPPLIES

**Cardstock:** (white) **Patterned paper:** (Buttercup/Sunshiney from Homespun collection) *Bo-Bunny Press*; (Splash from All About Boys collection) *Creative Imaginations*; (Textured Orange) *Scissor Sisters* **Accent:** (metal tag sentiment) *K&Company* **Fibers:** (white twill ribbon) *Creative Impressions*; (white thread) **Adhesive:** foam squares

INSTRUCTIONS

❶ Make card from cardstock. ❷ Trim each patterned paper to 1" x 3½"; adhere to card. ❸ Zigzag- stitch paper seams. ❹ Thread twill ribbon through tag; knot. Adhere to card with foam squares.

## Hey There Sugar

Designer: Marla Bird

SUPPLIES

**Textured cardstock:** (Walnut) *Bazzill Basics Paper*
**Patterned paper:** (Garden Rectangled) *KI Memories*
**Accent:** (sentiment die cut) *Provo Craft* **Fibers:**
(pink ribbon) *Ampelco* **Adhesive:** foam tape

### ADD SOME FLAVOR

*Try adding fabrics, ribbon, or buttons to your
design to spice up the recipe. This will give the card
a more visually interesting appearance.*

## Spring Tag

Designer: Kathleen Paneitz

SUPPLIES

**Patterned paper:** (Lime Dotted Check) *Karen
Foster Design*; (Pink Argyle) *Rusty Pickle*
**Accents:** (chipboard coaster) *Li'l Davis Designs*;
(silver wire clip) *Design Originals*; (decorative brad,
pink rivet) **Paper accents:** (pink and white paper
flowers) **Rub-on:** (sentiment) *Making Memories*
**Fibers:** (green argyle ribbon) *American Crafts*

MAKES ONE 4¾" x 3" TAG

## Sweet and Sassy Kid

Designer: Alisa Bangerter

SUPPLIES

**Textured cardstock:** (pink, dark pink) **Accent:**
(chipboard coaster) *Li'l Davis Designs* **Fibers:**
(black polka dot ribbon) *Offray*; (black thread)

## Love

Designer: Wendy Johnson

### SUPPLIES
*All supplies from K&Company unless otherwise noted.*
**Textured cardstock:** (Petalsoft) *Bazzill Basics Paper*
**Patterned paper:** (Madeira Wedding Border) **Accents:**
(love circle charm) **Fibers:** (pink ribbon)

### INSTRUCTIONS
❶ Make card from Petalsoft cardstock.
❷ Trim patterned paper slightly smaller than card; adhere. ❸ Cut slit on card fold; thread ribbon through slit.
❹ Adhere charm.

## Shopping with Friends

Designer: Wendy Sue Anderson

SUPPLIES
**Textured cardstock:** (Romance) *Bazzill Basics Paper* **Patterned paper:** (Pink Yellow Stripes) *Cross My Heart* **Accents:** (purse charm, rhinestones) **Fibers:** (pink polka dot, pink ribbon) *May Arts*

## Stripes and Daisies

Designer: Michelle Tardie

SUPPLIES
**Patterned paper:** (Stylin Stems, Garden Gossip from Aunt Gerti's Garden collection) *SEI* **Accent:** (tag) *SEI* **Fibers:** (green ribbon) *Offray*

## Spent My Money

Designer: Alice Golden

SUPPLIES
**Patterned paper:** (Lemonade from Sublime collection) *BasicGrey* **Dye ink:** (Peeled Paint) *Ranger Industries* **Accents:** (maroon round, tan square brads) *K&Company* **Paper accent:** (orange flower) *Prima* **Sticker:** (sentiment) **Fibers:** (twine)

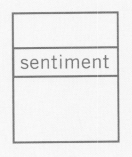

## Dad

Designer: Amber Crosby

### SUPPLIES

**Cardstock:** (Natural) *Bazzill Basics Paper* **Textured cardstock:** (Walnut) *Bazzill Basics Paper* **Patterned paper:** (Dandy Dots, Brilliant Beads from Peachy Keen collection) *Keeping Memories Alive* **Accents:** (label holder) *Making Memories*; (silver brads) *Impress Rubber Stamps* **Fibers:** (brown gingham ribbon) *Impress Rubber Stamps* **Font:** (Garamond) *Microsoft*

### INSTRUCTIONS

❶ Make card from Walnut cardstock. ❷ Trim Dandy Dots paper to ¾" x 3"; adhere to card. ❸ Trim Brilliant Beads paper to 1¾" x 3"; adhere to card. Adhere ribbon to paper seams. ❹ Print "Dad" on Natural cardstock; trim to fit label holder and adhere to card. ❺ Attach label holder over text with brads.

## Celebrate

Designer: Alisa Bangerter

SUPPLIES
**Cardstock:** (cream) **Textured cardstock:** (light green, yellow) **Accents:** (sentiment labels) *K&Company* **Fibers:** (yellow rickrack) *Wrights*; (cream grosgrain ribbon) *Making Memories* **Adhesive:** (pop-up dot) *Plaid*

## Tricks and Treats Gift Bag

Designer: Wendy Johnson

SUPPLIES
**Gift bag; Cardstock:** (purple) **Patterned paper:** (Wicked Stripes from Halloween collection) *Creative Imaginations* **Accents:** (sentiment) *Go West Studios*; (caramel candies) *EK Success* **Fibers:** (black rickrack) *Wrights Co.*

MAKES ONE 4" x 3¼" BAG

## Hugs and Kisses

Designer: Marla Bird

SUPPLIES
**Textured cardstock:** (Vanilla) *Bazzill Basics Paper* **Patterned paper:** (Pretty Crazy Ducky from She Wears Pink collection) *Imagination Project* **Accents:** (pink hinges, pink brads) *Making Memories* **Rub-ons:** (Heidi, mixed alphabet) *Making Memories* **Adhesive:** foam squares **Dies:** (Bounce alphabet) *Provo Craft/Ellison*

### SPICE IT UP
*Turn recipe parts into interactive elements for added dimension and fun.*

INSIDE FLAP

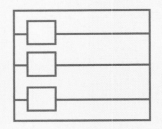

# Hello

Designer: Wendy Johnson

### SUPPLIES

**Cardstock:** (white) **Textured cardstock:** (Aloe Vera) *Bazzill Basics Paper* **Patterned paper:** (Circle Flowers from Dynamic collection, Orange Field from Wink collection) *Autumn Leaves* **Rub-on:** (Marmalade Small alphabet) *Doodlebug Design* **Stickers:** (flower epoxy) *Autumn Leaves* **Fibers:** (green ribbon) *Making Memories*; (orange striped ribbon) *Wrights*; (white rickrack) *Embellish It!*

### INSTRUCTIONS

❶ Make card from Aloe Vera cardstock. ❷ Cut strips of white cardstock and each patterned paper; adhere to card. ❸ Adhere ribbons and rickrack at paper seams. ❹ Add stickers; spell "Hello" with rub-ons.

### Father's Day Box

Designer: Kathleen Paneitz

SUPPLIES

**Box:** (White) *EK Success* **Patterned paper:** (Oxford Stripe, Urban Dot from Vagabond collection) *BasicGrey* **Accents:** (white hinges) *My Mind's Eye*; (metal ovals) *K&Company* **Rub-ons:** (Delineated, stamped alphabets) *Autumn Leaves*

MAKES ONE 2¼" x 3¼" x 3½" BOX

### Thank You Very Much

Designer: Susan Neal

SUPPLIES

**Cardstock:** (White) *Bazzill Basics Paper* **Textured cardstock:** (Petal Soft, Romance, Petunia, Sweetheart) *Bazzill Basics Paper* **Rubber stamps:** (Thank You Very Much) *Hero Arts* **Dye ink:** (Tea Dye) *Ranger Industries* **Pigment ink:** (Onyx Black) *Tsukineko* **Fibers:** (white thread) **Dies:** (mini hearts) *QuicKutz*

### Thank You, Dad

Designer: Alice Golden

SUPPLIES

**Cardstock:** (Birchstone Light, White Prismatic) *Karen Foster Design* **Patterned paper:** (Seine from Left Bank collection) *7gypsies* **Accents:** (metal index tabs) *7gypsies*; (thank you metal tag) *Making Memories* **Stickers:** (Stamp alphabet) *Creative Imaginations* **Tools:** (³⁄₁₆" circle punch)

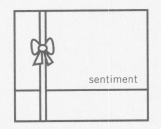

sentiment

## Mother in Pink

Designer: Wendy Johnson

SUPPLIES

**Cardstock:** (Green Galore) *Stampin' Up!*; (white)
**Patterned paper:** (Petal Pink) *Scissor Sisters*
**Accents:** (pink spiral clip) *Creative Expressions*;
(Limeade brads) *Doodlebug Design* **Stickers:** (epoxy
alphabet) *Autumn Leaves* **Fibers:** (white grosgrain
ribbon) *Michaels*; (white thread)

INSTRUCTIONS

❶ Make card from white cardstock.
❷ Trim rectangle of Green Galore cardstock; adhere to card. Trim strip of Petal
Pink paper; adhere to card. Stitch along
upper edge. ❸ Cut slit on card fold;
attach ribbon with spiral clip and brads.
❹ Apply stickers to spell "Mother"
on card.

### Love & Cherish

Designer: Alisa Bangerter

SUPPLIES

**Cardstock:** (Brick from Double-Dipped collection) *Making Memories*; (white) **Textured cardstock:** (Sage Green) *DMD, Inc.* **Accents:** (plastic tags) *Pebbles Inc.* **Rub-ons:** (sentiment) *Deja Views* **Fibers:** (sheer burgundy ribbon) *Offray* **Other:** sandpaper

### Thoughtful Get Well

Designer: Kathleen Paneitz

SUPPLIES

**Cardstock:** (white) **Patterned paper:** (Girly Stripes, Multistripes from Simply Chic collection) *American Crafts* **Accent:** (metal sentiment round) *Magic Scraps* **Rub-ons:** (sentiment) *Making Memories* **Fibers:** (pink ribbon) *Making Memories*

#### SPICE IT UP

*Create an optical illusion! Use vertical stripes and place the sentiment below the center line. The card will look taller than it really is.*

### New Baby!

Designer: Jana Millen

SUPPLIES

**Cardstock:** (white) **Textured cardstock:** (Baby Blue) *Bazzill Basics Paper* **Patterned paper:** (Boy Oh Boy Stripe/Blue, Boy Oh Boy Gingham/Tan) *My Mind's Eye* **Rubber stamp:** (New Baby) *Hero Arts* **Dye ink:** (Van Dyke Brown) *Ranger Industries* **Accent:** (safety pin charm) **Fibers:** (tan gingham ribbon) *Midori;* (white thread)

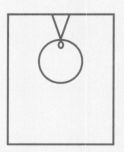

## One of a Kind

Designer: Linda Beeson

### SUPPLIES

**Textured cardstock:** (Blossom) *Bazzill Basics Paper* **Patterned paper:** (Floral Crochet Cream) *Sandylion* **Paper accent:** (mini tag) *Sandylion* **Accent:** (pink button) *Bazzill Basics Paper* **Rub-ons:** (1730 alphabet) *Autumn Leaves* **Fibers:** (pink polka dot ribbon) *May Arts*

### INSTRUCTIONS

❶ Make card from cardstock. ❷ Trim patterned paper to cover card back and form triangle flap over card front; adhere. ❸ Mat mini tag with cardstock. ❹ Attach ribbon through button and mini tag; tie bow. Adhere button to card. ❺ Spell "You" with rub-ons on card.

## Sweet Baby Rattle Tag

Designer: Wendy Johnson

SUPPLIES

**Cardstock:** (white) **Patterned paper:** (Sweet Baby Girl from Baby Girl Paper & Pieces Tablet) *Deja Views* **Paper accents:** (green round die cut, green scalloped border die cut) *Deja Views* **Accents:** (plastic keepsake pocket) *Pebbles Inc.*; (pastel beads) **Fibers:** (white ribbon, pink pompom cording) *May Arts*; (white twine, sheer green ribbon)

MAKES ONE 3¼" x 4¾" TAG

## No One Measures up to You

Designer: Sande Krieger

SUPPLIES

**Patterned paper:** (Scrappin' Brown, Rulers) *Design Originals* **Accents:** (copper antique button brad) *K&Company*; (copper overall clip) **Fibers:** (cream twill ribbon, rust thread)

## Great Getaway Luggage Tag

Designer: Michelle Tardie

SUPPLIES

**Textured cardstock:** (Suede Brown Medium) *Prism* **Patterned paper:** (Scratched Orange) *Karen Foster Design* **Pigment ink:** (Black) *Clearsnap* **Accent:** (silver bead chain) *Pebbles Inc.* **Sticker:** (travel phrase) *Karen Foster Design*

MAKES ONE 3" x 3½" TAG

# Christmas Bell

Designer: Wendy Johnson

SUPPLIES

**Cardstock:** (Black Holly) *Zim's* **Accent:** (plastic tag) *Doodlebug Design* **Fibers:** (green striped ribbon) *May Arts*; (red grosgrain ribbon) *Offray*; (brown ribbon, black thread) **Other:** sandpaper

MAKES ONE 3¼" x 3⅛" CARD

INSTRUCTIONS

❶ Make card from Black Holly cardstock; sand. ❷ Loop ribbons; adhere to card. ❸ Stitch tag to card.

## To Have & to Hold Booklet

Designer: Alisa Bangerter

SUPPLIES
**Cardstock:** (white) **Patterned paper:** (Silver Wedding) *Masterpiece Studios* **Accents:** (white flower button) *Blumenthal Lansing Co.*; (silver plastic wedding rings) *Michaels* **Fibers:** (silver ribbon, silver striped ribbon, white tulle net)

MAKES ONE 4½" x 4" BOOKLET

### TIP A LA ALISA
*When buying a wedding present with several other people, this booklet makes the perfect gift card. Everyone will have enough room to add their advice and best wishes for the bride and groom!*

## Celebrate Liberty Invitation

Designer: Marla Bird

SUPPLIES
**Cardstock:** (brown) **Textured cardstock:** (Red, Blue) *Bazzill Basics Paper* **Rubber stamps:** (Antique Lower Case alphabet) *Duncan* **Foam stamps:** (Jersey LC alphabet) *Making Memories* **Paint:** (Black) *Delta* **Dye Ink:** (brown) **Accent:** (metal jump ring) *ACCO* **Rub-ons:** (sentiment) *Making Memories*; (All Mixed Up medium alphabet) *Doodlebug Design* **Fibers:** (red grosgrain, blue striped, polka dot ribbon) *American Crafts*

MAKES ONE 4¼" SQUARE CARD

OPEN

## Thanks Teacher! Tag

Designer: Dee Gallimore-Perry

SUPPLIES
**Cardstock:** (Ginger, Black, White) *Bazzill Basics Paper* **Patterned paper:** (Black Alphabet) *Sweetwater* **Color medium:** (white pencil) *EK Success* **Accent:** (white safety pin) *Making Memories* **Sticker:** (Teacher) *Sweetwater* **Fibers:** (black and white gingham ribbon) *Offray*; (red printed ribbon) *Making Memories* **Tools:** (circle punch) *Emagination Crafts*

MAKES ONE 4¼" SQUARE TAG

### TIP A LA DEE
*This tag is a great way to say goodbye to a beloved teacher at the end of the year. Let your child write the sentiment and decoration on the "chalkboard" block.*

## Happy Day

Designer: Wendy Johnson

### SUPPLIES

**Cardstock:** (white) **Patterned paper:** (Colorful Rings from Surf's Up collection) *Treehouse Designs* **Accent:** (greeting round tile) *EK Success* **Fibers:** (yellow rickrack) *Wrights*; (blue gingham ribbon) *Offray*

### INSTRUCTIONS

❶ Make card from cardstock. ❷ Cut two strips of patterned paper; adhere to card. ❸ Adhere rickrack along seams. ❹ Thread ribbon through accent; knot. Adhere accent to card.

## Thinking of You

Designer: Alisa Bangerter

SUPPLIES

**Textured cardstock:** (Olive Green) *Die Cuts With a View* **Patterned paper:** (Flip Flop Stripe) *The Robin's Nest*; (Kiwi) *Scissor Sisters* **Accent:** (iron-on flower) *Hirschberg Schutz & Co.* **Rub-ons:** (sentiment) *K&Company* **Fibers:** (green trim) *May Arts* **Other:** sandpaper

## Boo!

Designer: Nichole Heady

SUPPLIES

**Cardstock:** (white) **Textured cardstock:** (green) **Patterned paper:** (Beach House Orange) *Rusty Pickle* **Foam craft sheet:** (white) **Rubber stamp:** (Pumpkin from Say It Simply set) *Stampin' Up!* **Color medium:** (Mellow Moss, Only Orange chalk) *Stampin' Up!* **Fibers:** (green stitched ribbon) *Morex Corp.*; (white floss) *DMC* **Tools:** (postage stamp decorative-edge scissors) *Fiskars*

### APPETIZING IDEA

*Add dimension to your cards with foam! Trim the edges with decorative scissors, then simply heat the foam and press a stamp into it, holding until the foam cools. Chalk the impression for a beautiful, colorful finish.*

## Thanks

Designer: Kathleen Paneitz

SUPPLIES

**Cardstock:** (white) **Patterned paper:** (Spring Polka Dot) *My Mind's Eye*; (Family Polka Stripes) *Carolee's Creations* **Accent:** (acrylic frame) *KI Memories* **Rub-ons:** (sentiment) *Making Memories*

## Miss You

Designer: Heather D. White

### SUPPLIES

**Patterned paper:** (Diamonds, Stripes from Day Spa collection) *Fancy Pants Designs* **Dye ink:** (Van Dyke Brown) *Ranger Industries* **Paper accents:** (blue, green flowers) *Fancy Pants Designs* **Accents:** (sentiment label) *Making Memories*; (white mini brads) *Karen Foster Design*

### INSTRUCTIONS

❶ Make card from Diamonds paper; ink edges. ❷ Trim strip of Stripes paper; ink edges. Adhere to card. ❸ Attach flowers to block with brads. ❹ Adhere label to card with brads. Adhere label to card.

### SECRET INGREDIENTS

*Instead of using cardstock to form a card, go ahead and create a card from patterned paper. Trim a block of the same paper to fit the cover, which keeps the card from being too flimsy as well as hides the backs of brads or stitching.*

## You Are Groovy

Designer: Sande Krieger

SUPPLIES

**Textured cardstock:** (white) **Paper accents:** (cardstock tags) *Making Memories* **Accents:** (silver, black brad) *Making Memories* **Rub-ons:** (Evolution alphabet) *Making Memories*; (Librarie Lettres alphabet) *7gypsies* **Fibers:** (black and white striped ribbon) *May Arts*

**TIP A LA SANDE**

*Don't throw away your scraps! Leftover white cardstock and extra black rub-ons look fantastic together. So use those extra bits and pieces to make fast and easy gift cards.*

## It's All in the Hat-titude!

Designer: Alisa Bangerter

SUPPLIES

**Cardstock:** (Grape from Double-Dipped collection) *Making Memories*; (white) **Textured cardstock:** (red) **Rubber stamp:** (Hat from A Little Love set) *Stampin' Up!* **Pigment ink:** (Red) *Tsukineko* **Embossing powder:** (Ruby Red) *Stampendous!* **Accents:** (stone tiles) *EK Success*; (red staples) *Making Memories* **Fibers:** (sheer purple, red ribbon) *Offray* **Font:** (CK Retro Block) *Creating Keepsakes* **Other:** sandpaper

**ADD SOME FLAVOR**

*The possibilities are endless for fun sentiments that match the stamp. Try "Hatty Birthday" or "Hats Off to You." Or, use a strawberry stamp for a "Have a Berry Good Day" card.*

## Antique Congratulations

Designer: Michelle Tardie

SUPPLIES

**Textured cardstock:** (Candle Glow Dark) *Prism* **Patterned paper:** (Vigne, French Stripe from French Market collection) *Daisy D's* **Accents:** (antique copper decorative brads) *Making Memories* **Rub-ons:** (sentiment) *Karen Foster Design*

## Best Friends Notebook

Designer: Wendy Johnson

SUPPLIES

**Mini composition book; Cardstock:** (white, pink) **Patterned paper:** (Coastline Fuchsia Bikini) *Making Memories* **Accents:** (orange buttons) *Blumenthal Lansing Co.* **Fibers:** (orange/pink ribbon) *Morex Corp.*; (pink gingham ribbon) *Offray*; (white rickrack) *Wrights*; (white floss) **Font:** (Typo) *www.twopeasinabucket.com* **Tool:** corner rounder punch

# CHAPTER 5

# Sweet Sampler

Sample the unique card designs in this chapter. With

fabulous folds, appetizing pull-outs, and fancy shapes,

these recipes are just right for any sweet occasion!

## Pocketful of Moods Album

Designer: Susan Neal

### SUPPLIES

**Cardstock:** (white, black) **Patterned paper:** (Pink Lady, Block Head, New Wheat, Waffle Board, Collage, Variegated Stripe from Sophie collection) *BasicGrey* **Dye ink:** (Tea Dye) *Ranger Industries* **Accent:** (round deco brad) *Making Memories*; (black matte brad) *Lasting Impressions for Paper* **Fibers:** (black elastic cord) *7gypsies*; (sheer white, pink and black ribbon; white thread) **Font:** (Trubble) *www.searchfreefonts.com* **Adhesive:** foam squares **Tools:** circle, flower punch

MAKES ONE 4¼" x 4¾" x ¾" ALBUM

### PREPARATION

❶ Cut album cover and pages, following pattern on p. 180. ❷ Cut pieces of all patterned paper; adhere to all sides of cover and pages. Stitch paper seams and border on cover; stitch tops of pages. *Note: Fold page pieces to create four pages.*

### COVER

❶ Print "mma's" on white cardstock; trim, ink, and adhere to cover. ❷ Print "E" on white; trim, ink, and mat with black cardstock circle. Adhere to cover. ❸ Print "Pocketful of moods" on white; ink and adhere with foam squares. Print mood definition on white; ink and tie knot. Slip underneath title sentiment. ❹ Punch flower from New Wheat paper; ink edges and attach with brad. ❺ Punch hole on back cover of album; thread loop of elastic cord through and knot to secure. *Note: Close album by hooking elastic loop around brad on front cover.*

### INSIDE PAGE

❶ Print information about recipient on white; trim, ink, and mat with black. Adhere inside front cover. ❷ Trim photo; adhere to page. ❸ Print mood definition on white; ink and adhere to page. ❹ Punch flower from New Wheat; ink edges and attach to page with matte brad.

### ASSEMBLY

❶ Punch two sets of holes in book spine. ❷ Fold pages in half; attach by tying ribbon around them and through holes in spine. ❸ Tie ribbons together into bow.

**TIP A LA SUSAN**

*Take multiple pictures of the recipient, and experiment with cropping to find the right look for each mood. For instance, use a beautiful smile to illustrate joy or happiness, or downcast eyes to depict a person's shy or quiet side.*

INSIDE

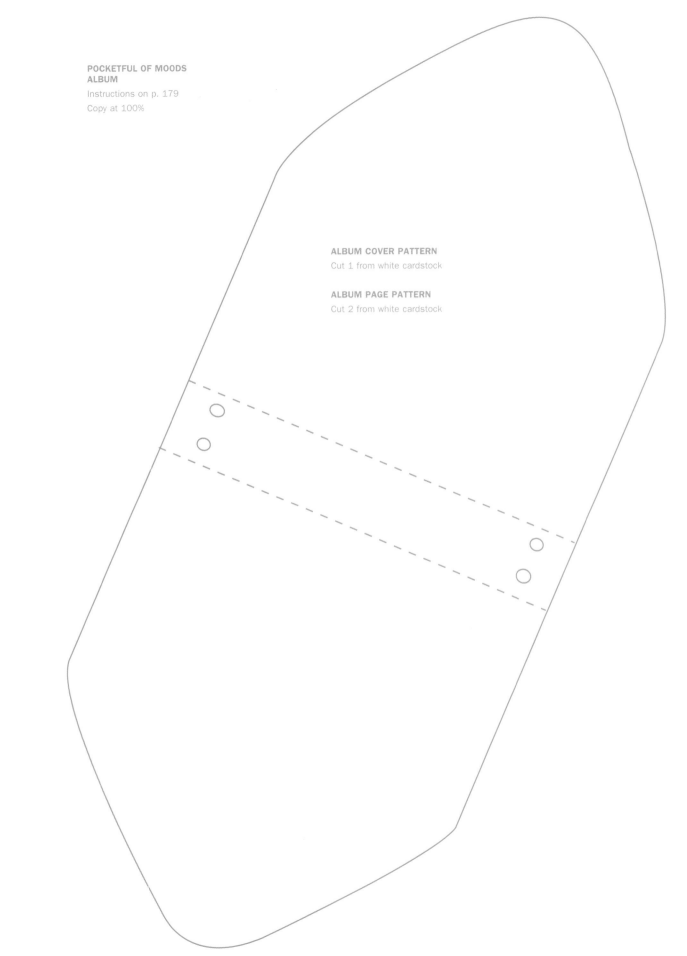

POCKETFUL OF MOODS
ALBUM
Instructions on p. 179
Copy at 100%

ALBUM COVER PATTERN
Cut 1 from white cardstock

ALBUM PAGE PATTERN
Cut 2 from white cardstock

## Festive Birthday Gift Bag

Designer: Wendy Sue Anderson

SUPPLIES

**Gift bag:** (lime green) *DMD, Inc.* **Textured cardstock:** (Pink, Yellow) *Die Cuts With a View* **Paper accents:** (multicolored gift shred) *DMD, Inc.* **Accent:** (birthday label) *Making Memories* **Font:** (Uncle Charles) *Autumn Leaves* **Adhesive:** foam squares

MAKES ONE 5¼" x 8½" BAG

### TIP A LA WENDY SUE

*Tuck a matching gift card or two in the pocket for an added birthday bonus.*

## Father's Day Wishes

Designer: Wendy Johnson

SUPPLIES

**Cardstock:** (blue, white) **Patterned paper:** (Fall Paisley/Brown) *My Mind's Eye* **Accent:** (bronze fastener) *Rusty Pickle* **Fibers:** (linen thread) *Stampin' Up!*; (brown thread) **Font:** (Flower Pot) *www.twopeasinabucket.com*

MAKES ONE 4½" x 4¼" CARD

### APPETIZING IDEAS

*Try changing the size of this recipe to create a larger card with room for lots of text, or a smaller card to attach to a gift.*

*This card's fold is at the top, but you can also make it with a side fold for added variation.*

*Use patterned paper reminiscent of Dad's favorite pair of pants or work shirt.*

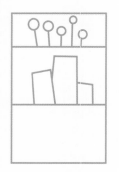

## Get Well Pockets

Designer: Wendy Johnson

SUPPLIES

**Cardstock:** (white, olive, red) **Patterned paper:** (Summer Rays, Thyme and Again) *Provo Craft*; (Summer Stripe) *Daisy D's* **Accents:** (yellow flower) *Making Memories*; (flower charm, mini clothespin) **Fasteners:** (antique brad, antique decorative brad, eyelet) *Making Memories* **Fibers:** (red gingham ribbon) *Li'l Davis Designs*; (green ribbon) *Making Memories* **Fonts:** (Picnic Basket, 2Ps Sunshine) www.twopeasinabucket.com **Adhesive:** (glue stick) **Tools:** (Folk Heart, Bitsy Circle, Flower punches) Paper Shapers, *EK Success*; scissors, hole punch, ruler, sewing machine, computer and printer, eyelet-setting tools **Other:** wooden toothpick, cough drops, herbal tea packet, facial tissues, white thread

MAKES ONE 3⅝" x 7½" CARD

### MAKE CARD

❶ Make card from white cardstock, following instructions above. ❷ Trim Summer Rays paper to fit each panel; adhere. ❸ Machine-stitch along each open side to create pockets.

### EMBELLISH

❶ Print "for you" on white cardstock; trim and mat with olive cardstock. Adhere to toothpick. ❷ Punch out flower from red cardstock and circle from Summer Rays; adhere together and adhere to printed sign.

❸ Print "get well soon" on white; trim and mat with red. Adhere flower charm and attach sentiment on bottom pocket with mini clothespin, adhering in place. ❹ Trim Thyme and Again paper into tag; set eyelet at top and thread ribbon through. ❺ Trim Summer Stripe paper into tag; mat with red cardstock and attach ribbon and brad at top. ❻ Attach decorative brad to flower; adhere to striped tag. Place both tags in center pocket. ❼ Fill top pocket with facial tissues, tea packet, and cough drops; adhere "for you" sign.

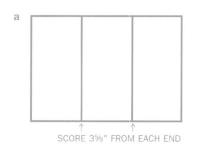

a

SCORE 3⅝" FROM EACH END

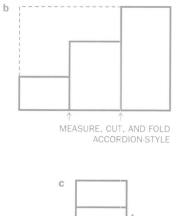

b

MEASURE, CUT, AND FOLD ACCORDION-STYLE

c

ADHERE OPEN ENDS

*These two pockets can be used for gift cards, money, bookmarks, tags, candy, or any other trinket or treasure. Use one to hold your message or sentiment.*

### INSTRUCTIONS

❶ Cut paper to 7½" x 11". ❷ Score at 3⅝" from each end (see Figure a). ❸ Cut and fold as shown in illustration (see Figure b). ❹ Adhere each flap on open side (see Figure c). ❺ Embellish as desired.

## The Kindness of Friends

**Designer: Michelle Tardie**

SUPPLIES

**Textured cardstock:** (Parakeet) *Bazzill Basics Paper* **Pigment ink:** (Black) ColorBox, *Clearsnap* **Patterned paper:** (Bluebell Gingham, Bluebell Map, Bluebell Vine) *Daisy D's* **Paper accents:** (script tag) *FooFaLa*; (manila tag) *Avery Dennison* **Accent:** (spiral clip) *Target* **Stickers:** (stitched flower, tulips, button quote from Simple Joys set) Stick-Its, *O'Scrap!*; (friend, kindness, respect) *Tumblebeasts* **Fibers:** (Butterscotch check) *Lifetime Moments* **Adhesive:** (glue stick) **Tools:** scissors

MAKES ONE 3⅝" x 7½" CARD

## Congrats Grad

**Designer: Lori Allred**

SUPPLIES

Textured cardstock: (Raven, Ivory) *Bazzill Basics Paper*

**Patterned paper:** (Pinecone Gingham) *Bo-Bunny Press*; (B&W Alphabet) *Rusty Pickle* **Dye ink:** (black) *Walnut ink: Rusty Pickle* **Accent:** (spiral clip) *Making Memories* **Rub-ons:** (White Providence) Simply Stated Alphabet, *Making Memories* **Sticker:** (Success) Defined, *Making Memories* **Fasteners:** (pewter brads, black snap) *Making Memories* **Font:** (CK Regal) "Creative Clips & Fonts for Special Occasions" CD, *Creating Keepsakes* **Adhesive:** (glue stick) **Tools:** scissors, eyelet-setting tools, sponge

MAKES ONE 3⅝" x 7½" CARD

**QUOTE**

*"A graduation ceremony is an event where the commencement speaker tells thousands of students dressed in identical caps and gowns that 'individuality' is the key to success. Congratulations on your graduation!"*

## New Year's Wishes

**Designer: Nichole Heady**

SUPPLIES

**Cardstock:** (white) **Patterned paper:** (Blue, Green) *Robin's Nest*; (Water Mosaic) Collection II, *KI Memories* **Fasteners:** (star eyelets) *Stampin' Up!* **Fibers:** (silver cord) *Stampin' Up!* **Fonts:** (Futura Light) *Microsoft*; (CK Signature) "Creative Clips & Fonts by Becky Higgins" CD, *Creating Keepsakes* **Adhesive:** (glue stick) **Tools:** scissors, eyelet-setting tools, computer and printer

MAKES ONE 3⅝" x 7½" CARD

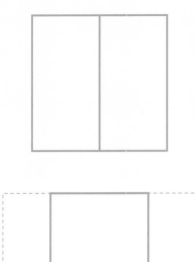

## F Is for Friend

Designer: Wendy Johnson

### SUPPLIES

**Textured cardstock:** (Raven) *Bazzill Basics Paper* **Patterned paper:** (Beach House Red, Anuenue Slices, Anuenue Leaf) *Rusty Pickle* **Foam stamps:** (Philadelphia Uppercase, Philadelphia Lowercase) *Making Memories*; (Jive Alphabet) Simply Stamps, *Plaid* **Accents:** ("F" tile) Paper Bliss, *Westrim Crafts*; (yellow daisy) *Making Memories*; (spiral clip) *7gypsies* **Stickers:** (Mixed Fruit alphabet) PureJuice, *Memories Complete* **Fasteners:** (green eyelets) *Prym-Dritz*; (brad) **Fibers:** (green polka-dot ribbon) *May Arts*; (white, black, yellow, green striped ribbon) *Making Memories* **Adhesive:** (glue stick) **Tools:** scissors, sewing machine, eyelet-setting tools, hole punch, paintbrush, ruler **Other:** white thread

MAKES ONE 6" SQUARE CARD

### INSTRUCTIONS

① Cut Raven cardstock to 12" x 6". Score 3" from left and right edges; fold to center of card. ② Cut two strips of each patterned paper; adhere to card. ③ Machine-stitch papers along seams; adhere black and white ribbons to card. ④ Fold green polka-dot ribbon into V and attach to flower accent with brad; adhere "F" tile to center of flower and adhere to card. ⑤ Adhere spiral clip near flower. ⑥ Spell "friends" with alphabet stickers on card. ⑦ Set eyelets in center of card, one on each flap; thread green striped and yellow ribbons through and tie closed.

*Adorn this card with a fun closure. Try ribbons, buttons, clasps, or hook and loop fasteners to keep the two panels closed. Be creative!*

### INSTRUCTIONS

① Cut card to desired size. ② Score card on each end so two sides meet in center when folded. ③ Embellish.

INSIDE

## A+ Teacher

Designer: Kathleen Paneitz

SUPPLIES

**Cardstock:** (white) **Patterned paper:** (School House) *Making Memories*; (Alphabet) Jenni Bowlin, *Li'l Davis Designs* **Color medium:** (black marker) ZIG Writer, *EK Success* **Paper accent:** (pencil) Jolee's by You, *EK Success* **Accents:** (rectangle metal-rimmed tag, jump ring) *Making Memories*; (apple button) Dress It Up, *Jesse James & Co.* **Stickers:** (rulers) Life's Journey, *K&Company*; (Martin Brush alphabet) Teri Martin, *Creative Imaginations* **Fasteners:** (washer eyelets) *Creative Impressions* **Fibers:** (black gingham ribbon) *Offray* **Font:** (CK Evolution) "CK Fresh Fonts" CD, *Creating Keepsakes* **Adhesive:** (glue stick) **Tools:** (label maker) *Dymo*; scissors, paper trimmer, eyelet-setting tools, computer and printer, black label tape

MAKES ONE 5" SQUARE CARD

## Mom

Designer: Dee Gallimore-Perry

SUPPLIES

**Textured cardstock:** (Pear) *Bazzill Basics Paper* **Patterned paper:** (Sand Light Plaid) *Kopp Design* **Paper accents:** (flowers from Cousins set) Dee's Designs, *My Mind's Eye* **Sticker:** (mom from Family set) Wonderful Words, *Déjà Views, C-Thru Ruler Co.* **Fasteners:** (white eyelets) **Fibers:** (olive, antique, green gingham) *Making Memories*

MAKES ONE 5½" SQUARE CARD

## All-Girl Party

Designer: Sande Krieger

SUPPLIES

**Patterned paper:** (Block Head-S, Variegated Stripe-S) Sophie Collection, *BasicGrey* **Paper accents:** (All Girl, For You) Alphadotz, *Scrapworks* **Accents:** (Antique Pink Playful Alphabet) *Li'l Davis Designs*; (flower charm) *Frost Creek Charms* **Fasteners:** (pink rivets) *Chatterbox* **Fibers:** (fabric scraps) *Jo-Ann Stores* **Adhesive:** (wood adhesive, glue stick) **Tools:** scissors, eyelet-setting tools, hole punch

MAKES ONE 6" SQUARE CARD

**TIPS A LA SANDE**

*Turn this into a fun invitation by printing party details on the inside.*

*Include a small charm for a simple gift.*

## Thank You Flower

Designer: Wendy Johnson

SUPPLIES

**Cardstock:** (white) **Patterned paper:** (Blue Splatter, Princess Pink Plaid) *Bo-Bunny Press* **Accent:** (Thank You Ice Candy) Collection III, *KI Memories*; (staple) *Making Memories* **Sticker:** (flower) Sticko, *EK Success* **Fasteners:** (pink brad) *Making Memories* **Fibers:** (blue gingham ribbon) *Offray* **Adhesive:** (glue stick) **Tools:** scissors, ruler, hole punch, stapler

MAKES ONE 3½" x 3¾" CARD

a

SCORE AND FOLD

*This oversized matchbook card is a fun and creative way to give a handmade greeting. Stitch or staple the bottom flap and tuck the top flap into it for a unique card that will make someone smile.*

INSTRUCTIONS

❶ Cut cardstock to 3¾" x 7¾". ❷ Score and fold as shown (see Figure a). ❸ Stitch or staple bottom flap in place, leaving a small lip to tuck in upper flap. ❹ Embellish as desired.

INSTRUCTIONS

❶ Make card from white cardstock, following directions above. ❷ Cut Princess Pink Plaid paper to 3½" x 3¼"; adhere to top flap. ❸ Cut Blue Splatter paper to ¾" x 3¼"; adhere to bottom flap. ❹ Staple bottom flap into place. ❺ Tuck top flap into bottom flap and adhere accent to bottom flap. ❻ Adhere ribbon and apply sticker; attach brad to center of flower.

## Happy Birthday Daisies

Designer: Nichole Heady

SUPPLIES

*All supplies from Stampin' Up! unless otherwise noted.*

**Cardstock:** (Bordering Blue, Mellow Moss, Ultrasmooth White) **Rubber stamps:** (solid flower from Fun With Shapes set, happy birthday from Little Hellos set, daisy block from Mostly Flowers set, French Script background) **Dye ink:** (Bordering Blue, Basic Black, Mellow Moss) Classic Stampin' Pad **Fasteners:** (Bordering Blue eyelets) **Fibers:** (Celery ribbon) **Adhesive:** (glue stick) no source **Tools:** (scissors, eyelet-setting tools) no source

## Get Well Wishes

Designer: Kathleen Paneitz

SUPPLIES

**Cardstock:** (white) **Patterned paper:** (Grasshopper/Limeade Bloomers) *Doodlebug Design*; (Subtle Green Stripe) *Paper fever* **Accents:** (green concho) Hugz, *Scrapworks* **Fasteners:** (washer eyelets) *Creative Impressions* **Fibers:** (green gingham ribbon) *Offray* **Font:** (2Ps Ragtag) *www.twopeasinabucket.com* **Adhesive:** (glue stick) **Tools:** (leaf #i186, flower #S841 templates) *Lasting Impressions for Paper*, (circle punch) *Paper Shapers*, *EK Success*; scissors, light box or sunny window, stylus, eyelet-setting tools, computer and printer

## Many Thanks

Designer: Lori Allred

SUPPLIES

**Textured cardstock:** (Ivory) Bazzill Basics Paper **Card:** (Meadow Random Stripe/Meadow) Matchbook Cards, *Making Memories* **Color medium:** (brown chalk) **Accents:** (thank you labels) Woven Labels, (staples) *Making Memories* **Fastener:** (pink brad) *Making Memories* **Fibers:** (green gingham, light green, pink gingham ribbons) *SEI* **Adhesive:** (glue stick) **Tools:** scissors, stapler, hole punch, chalk applicator

MAKES ONE 4¼" x 5½" CARD

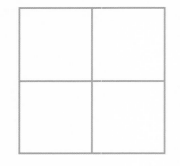

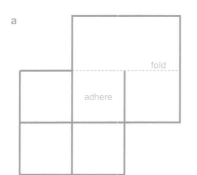

a

fold

adhere

ADHERE TWO SQUARES TOGETHER

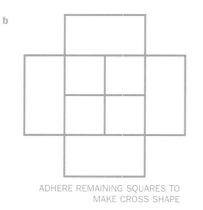

b

ADHERE REMAINING SQUARES TO
MAKE CROSS SHAPE

*This square card has four panels that fold into one
another. Embellish each square as desired, then lift
up the flaps to reveal your personal message!*

## INSTRUCTIONS

① Cut four 5" squares of cardstock. ② Score
each square through center and fold in half.
③ Adhere two squares together as shown
(see Figure a). ④ Adhere remaining two
squares to first two, to create cross shape
(see Figure b). ⑤ Fold each flap toward
center, overlapping corners to secure.
*Note: Alternate corner overlaps as if closing
a packing box without tape.* ⑥ Embellish
as desired.

# Four-Square Pumpkins

Designer: Wendy Johnson

SUPPLIES

**Cardstock:** (Tan) *SEI*; (olive, cream, dark brown) **Patterned paper:** (Squashed Pumpkin) *Provo Craft*;
(Orange Web) *Karen Foster Design*; (Fall Gingham) *Bo-Bunny Press*; (Brite Orange) Perky Plaids, *Keeping
Memories Alive* **Color medium:** (brown chalk) *Craf-T Products* **Accents:** (orange, yellow buttons) Dress
It Up, *Jesse James & Co.* **Fibers:** (green gingham ribbon) *Offray*; (orange striped ribbon) *May Arts*
**Font:** (Broken Flower Pot) *www.twopeasinabucket.com* **Adhesive:** (glue stick) **Tools:** scissors, hole punch,
computer and printer, chalk applicator **Other:** white thread, sandpaper, pencil
MAKES ONE 5¼" SQUARE CARD

## INSTRUCTIONS

① Make card from Tan cardstock, following
instructions above. ② Cut pumpkin from
each patterned paper; chalk edges, and
adhere one pumpkin to each small square
on front of card. ③ Cut four small rectangles of dark brown cardstock and adhere
one to each pumpkin for stem. Tie bows
and adhere to pumpkins. ④ Print "happy
halloween" on cream cardstock; chalk
edges, trim into shortened tag shape,
and mat with Orange Web paper and
olive cardstock. Punch hole at top.
⑤ String thread through buttons and
adhere to pumpkins. ⑥ Wrap ribbon
around outside of card; string through
tag and knot in center. ⑦ Mat card with
olive cardstock.

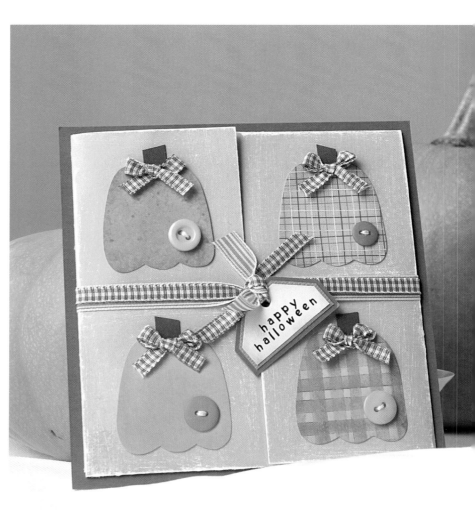

# Mother's Day Blossom

Designer: Wendy Sue Anderson

SUPPLIES
**Cardstock:** (Lemonade, Wheat, Windy, Pear)
*Bazzill Basics Paper* **Dye ink:** (Sand) Memories,
*Stewart Superior Corp.* **Rub-ons:** (Black Heidi)
Simply Stated Alphabets, *Making Memories*
**Stickers:** (flower, leaves, center from Simple Joys
Build-a-Flower set) *O'Scrap!* **Fibers:** (jute) **Tools:**
scissors, 1/16" hole punch

MAKES ONE 5¼" SQUARE CARD

---

### APPETIZING IDEAS
*Create this fun flower centerpiece by adhering
the die cut to one flap. When the flaps are closed,
the flower will be in the middle and secure the
card. Tie a jute bow to accent.*

---

# Spring Flowers

Designer: Lori Allred

SUPPLIES
**Textured cardstock:** (Purple Palisade, Blushing,
Butter Cream, Rainforest) *National Cardstock* **Dye
ink:** (brown) **Paper accents:** (Sampler Squares die
cuts) *Sweetwater* **Adhesive:** (glue stick) **Tools:**
square punch, scissors

MAKES ONE 5¼" SQUARE CARD

---

### SECRET INGREDIENTS
*For a softer inked look on cardstock, try using
a stipple brush and lightly "stamping" around
edges. It darkens the area more subtly and looks
fantastic on textured cardstock.*

---

# Birthday Wish

Designer: Dee Gallimore-Perry

SUPPLIES
**Cardstock:** (Bazzill White) *Bazzill Basics Paper*
**Patterned paper:** (Lipstick Flower, Birthday Word
Find, Birthday Dots, Birthday Barcode) Collection
III, *KI Memories* **Paper accents:** (Birthday Blox,
Birthday Circle Tags, Birthday Frames, Bright
Greetings Frames) Collection III, *KI Memories*
**Accents:** (watch crystal) *Deluxe Plastic Arts*; (seed
beads, mini clothespin) **Fibers:** (blue gingham rib-
bon) *Impress Rubber Stamps* **Adhesive:** (liquid
adhesive) KI Gloo, *KI Memories*; (foam tape)
**Tools:** scissors

MAKES ONE 5¼" SQUARE CARD

---

### TIPS A LA DEE
*To save time, make this card from white
cardstock first. Adhere patterned paper
rectangles to flaps, then tuck in to secure.
Embellish each square with ease!*

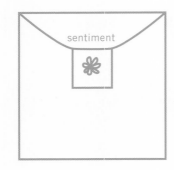

## Springtime Friends

Designer: Wendy Johnson

SUPPLIES
**Cardstock:** (olive) **Patterned paper:** (Daffodil Plaid, Daisy) *K&Company* **Sticker:** (Friends) *K&Company*
**Fibers:** (green grosgrain ribbon) *Making Memories* **Adhesive:** (glue stick) **Tools:** scissors, bone folder
MAKES ONE 5" x 4½" CARD

INSTRUCTIONS

❶ Make card from olive cardstock, following instructions above. ❷ Cut Daffodil Plaid paper to fit large front flap; adhere. ❸ Cut Daisy paper to fit smaller flap and back of card; adhere. *Note: Trim Daisy paper slightly smaller than flap to leave olive cardstock edge.* ❹ Adhere ribbon around card; tie bow. ❺ Apply sticker to smaller flap.

a

SCORE 4½" FROM ONE EDGE AND 2"
FROM OPPOSITE EDGE

*This tri-fold card is sealed with an embellishment. Place the sentiment on the flap above for a cool, creative look.*

INSTRUCTIONS

❶ Cut cardstock to 5" x 11". ❷ Score as shown (see Figure a). ❸ Cut corners off smaller flap. ❹ Fold and embellish.

## All I Am

Designer: Sande Krieger

SUPPLIES

**Patterned paper:** (Peach Melba Stripes) *Scenic Route Paper Co.* **Accent:** (flower) *Making Memories* **Rub-on:** (All I am from Mother set) Simple Thoughts Series 2, *Cloud 9 Design* **Fastener:** (antique brad) *Creative Impressions* **Tools:** scissors

MAKES ONE 5" x 4½" CARD

## Birthday Girl

Designer: Michelle Tardie

SUPPLIES

**Textured cardstock:** (Bubble Gum, Bazzill White, Olive) *Bazzill Basics Paper* **Paper accent:** (Birthday Girl from Party set) Embossible Designs, *We R Memory Keepers* **Fibers:** (white floss) *DMC* **Adhesive:** (glue stick) **Tools:** scissors, hole punch

MAKES ONE 5" x 4½" CARD

### SECRET INGREDIENTS

*Create the look of matting by adhering thin strips of paper or cardstock along edges of flaps. It adds a subtle touch of interest to any card project!*

## Welcome to the Neighborhood

Designer: Wendy Sue Anderson

SUPPLIES

**Cardstock:** (Cajun) *Bazzill Basics Paper* **Patterned paper:** (Powder Blossoms, Light Powder Stripe) Powder Room Collection, *Chatterbox* **Dye ink:** (Black) Memories, *Stewart Superior Corp.* **Paper accent:** (house) Paper Bliss, *Westrim Crafts* **Stickers:** (Rain Drop alphabet) Déjà Views, *C-Thru Ruler Company* **Adhesive:** (glue stick) **Tools:** scissors, paper trimmer, sewing machine, bone folder **Other:** white thread

MAKES ONE 5" x 4½" CARD

sentiment

## Pink and Blue Birthday

Designer: Wendy Johnson

### SUPPLIES

**Cardstock:** (white) **Patterned paper:** (Sugar and Spice, Tiny Mosaic Pink) *Paper fever*, (Pineapple) *Making Memories* **Accents:** (blue, green, yellow, white, pink buttons) *Making Memories* **Rub-ons:** (happy, birthday) Simply Stated, *Making Memories* **Fastener:** (pink eyelet) *Making Memories* **Fibers:** (pink cord, blue gingham ribbon, white ribbon) *Making Memories* **Adhesive:** (glue stick) **Tools:** (daisy punch) *Stampin' Up!*; (scissors, eyelet-setting tools, hole punch)

MAKES ONE 3½" x 5" CARD

*Make this fun and simple tag to attach to a gift, or just as a card.*

### INSTRUCTIONS

❶ Cut cardstock to 3½" x 10". ❷ Score and fold in half. ❸ Trace tag pattern with top of tag along fold; cut out. ❹ Embellish as desired.

### INSTRUCTIONS

❶ Make card from white cardstock, following instructions at left. ❷ Cut Sugar and Spice paper to fit tag front; adhere. ❸ Cut strip of Tiny Mosaic Pink paper, mat with Pineapple, and tear matted edges; adhere to tag. ❹ Punch daisy from white cardstock; adhere ribbon, buttons, and daisy to tag. ❺ Apply rub-ons; punch hole at top, set eyelet, and tie ribbons through hole.

# Shockingly Normal

Designer: Lori Allred

SUPPLIES

**Textured cardstock:** (Lemonade) *Bazzill Basics Paper* **Patterned paper:** (Light Powder Plaid) Powder Room Collection, *Chatterbox* **Accent:** (pink button) *SEI* **Fibers:** (pink ribbon) *SEI*; (yellow floss) *DMC* **Font:** (CK Regal) "Creative Clips & Fonts for Special Occasions" CD, *Creating Keepsakes* **Adhesive:** (glue stick) **Tools:** scissors, computer and printer

MAKES ONE 3½" x 5" CARD

# Phenomenal, Funny Father

Designer: Michelle Tardie

SUPPLIES

**Textured cardstock:** (Lighthouse) *Bazzill Basics Paper* **Patterned paper:** (Dark Den Circles) Den Collection, *Chatterbox* **Paper accents:** (Den tag, Den frames, Den molding) Den Collection, *Chatterbox* **Stickers:** (phenomenal, funny, father) Book Cloth, *Chatterbox* **Fastener:** (blue brad) *Karen Foster Design* **Fibers:** (navy twill) Twill E Dee, *Creek Bank Creations* **Adhesive:** (glue stick, foam tape) **Tools:** (decorative-edge scissors) *Fiskars*; (scissors, ¼" hole punch, ¹⁄₁₆" hole punch)

MAKES ONE 3⅛" x 5⅛" CARD

# Happy Winter

Designer: Nichole Heady

SUPPLIES

**Cardstock:** (Real Red, Old Olive, Naturals Ivory) *Stampin' Up!* **Rubber stamps:** (snowflakes from It's Snow Time set, happy winter from Flexible Phrases set, Simple Stripes background) *Stampin' Up!* **Dye ink:** (Real Red, Chocolate Chip) Classic Stampin' Pad, *Stampin' Up!* **Watermark ink:** VersaMark, *Tsukineko* **Accent:** (mitten) *Wimpole Street Creations* **Fibers:** (red grosgrain ribbon) *Stampin' Up!* **Adhesive:** (dots) *Glue Dots International*; (glue stick) **Tools:** scissors, hole punch

MAKES ONE 3½" x 5" CARD

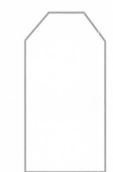

## Best Friend Blossom

Designer: Wendy Johnson

SUPPLIES

**Cardstock:** (Blue) *One Heart...One Mind*; (white) **Textured cardstock:** (Celery) *Bazzill Basics Paper* **Patterned paper:** (Cole from Melissa Frances collection) *Heart and Home* **Paper accent:** (flower die cut) *My Mind's Eye* **Accents:** (acrylic round) *KI Memories*; (woven alphabet labels) *Colorbok* **Fibers:** (pink and white ribbon) *Embellish It!*; (blue and white ribbon) *Offray*; (green grosgrain ribbon) *Michaels*; (white ribbon)

MAKES ONE 4" x 7½" CARD

INSTRUCTIONS

❶ Make card from white cardstock; trim top corners into tag shape. ❷ Cut Celery cardstock to fit card front; adhere. ❸ Cut Cole paper and Blue cardstock to fit card front; tear bottom edges, layer, and adhere. ❹ Adhere acrylic round and die cut to card. ❺ Spell "Friend" with alphabet labels. ❻ Punch holes at top of card; knot ribbon through.

## Father's Day Accordion Card

Designer: JoAnne Bacon

SUPPLIES
**Cardstock:** (white) **Patterned paper:** (Scarlet Bandana, Olive Bandana, Vest Stripe, Knicker Stripe from Great Room collection; Chocolate Ivy from Gallery collection) *Chatterbox* **Photos; Accents:** (antique rivets) *Marcella by Kay for Target;* (antique Snaps) *Chatterbox* **Fibers:** (red velvet, brown ribbon) *SEI*

MAKES ONE 3½"" x 6" CLOSED CARD
OPEN 10½" x 6"

### TIP A LA JOANNE
*To create the accordion card, fold an 8½" x 11" paper into three equal sections, accordion-style, and trim the top of each panel into a tag shape.*

## Haunted Headstone Invitation

Designer: Alisa Bangerter

SUPPLIES
**Cardstock:** (gray speckled) **Patterned paper:** (Farmhouse Black) *Rusty Pickle* **Vellum:** (white, orange, green) **Foam stamps:** (Jersey alphabet) *Making Memories* **Paint:** (Black) *Delta* **Accents:** (brass safety pin) *Making Memories;* (plastic spiders) **Fibers:** (black gingham ribbon) *Offray* **Font:** (CK Inky) *Creating Keepsakes* **Adhesive:** (pop-up dots) *Plaid*

MAKES ONE 4" x 8½" TAG

## Love to Keep Me Warm

Designer: Nichole Heady

SUPPLIES
**Cardstock:** (cream) **Patterned paper:** (Christmas Snowflakes) *K&Company;* (red polka dot) **Rubber stamp:** (love from Wonderful Words set) *Stampin'*

Up! **Dye ink:** (Real Red) *Stampin' Up!* **Accents:** (heart button) *Jesse James & Co.;* (red coat) *EK Success* **Fibers:** (red striped ribbon) *Morex Corp.;* (white floss) **Font:** (Bernhard Mod BT) *Microsoft* **Tools:** (scallop decorative-edge scissors)

MAKES ONE 4" x 8½" CARD

REVERSE

...to a
SPOOKTACULAR
Party!

October 31st
7:00 p.m. - 1:00 a.m.
Jones backyard

Lots of
tricks and treats

Come if you dare!

OPEN

Happy    Father's    Day!

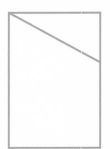

## Door to My Heart

Designer: Wendy Johnson

### SUPPLIES

**Cardstock:** (Peanut) *Bazzill Basics Paper*; (white)
**Patterned paper:** (Aged Barn Red) *Scissor Sisters* **Color medium:** (brown chalk) *Craf-T Products* **Paper accents:** (chipboard letters) *Rusty Pickle* **Accents:** (metal heart) *Pressed Petals*; (door handle) *7gypsies*; (key) *Making Memories* **Fibers:** (brown and black ribbon) *Making Memories* **Font:** (Notnorvalhmk) *Hallmark*

MAKES ONE 5" x 8" CARD

### INSTRUCTIONS

❶ Make card from white cardstock.
❷ Cut Aged Barn Red paper to fit card front; adhere. ❸ Cut front flap on slant from fold. ❹ Adhere chipboard letters to spell "Love". ❺ Knot ribbon on key; adhere key and door handle to card.
❻ Cut Peanut cardstock to fit inside card; chalk edges and adhere. ❼ Print "Door to my heart" on white; chalk edges and trim into strip. ❽ Adhere metal heart inside card with printed strip and strips of Aged Barn Red and Peanut (see photo).

## Reasons I Adore You Album

Designer: Susan Neal

SUPPLIES
**Cardstock:** (Stonehenge, Black) *Bazzill Basics Paper* **Textured cardstock:** (Sienna) *Bazzill Basics Paper* **Patterned paper:** (Red Damask from Brianna collection; Script) *K&Company* **Photos Rubber stamps:** (Knockout Alphabet) *Hampton Art*; (Circle Pop Alphabet, Pastel Pop Alphabet) *Hero Arts*; (Antique UC Alphabet, Antique LC Alphabet) *Duncan* **Pigment ink:** (Vintage Sepia, Onyx Black) *Tsukineko* **Accents:** (metal quotes) *Making Memories*; (staple) **Fibers:** (rust ribbon) **Dies:** (heart) *QuicKutz*

MAKES ONE 3¾" x 6" CLOSED ALBUM
OPEN 11¼" x 6"

**TIP A LA SUSAN**
*This variation on the recipe was created by using a tri-fold on the main piece. The booklet is held closed by a removable strip.*

INSIDE

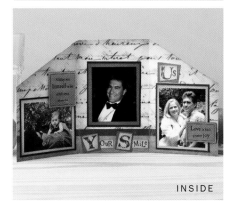

INSIDE

## Bon Voyage

Designer: Alice Golden

SUPPLIES
**Cardstock:** (Tsumugi Turquoise) *Hanko Designs* **Patterned paper:** (Tropical Beach) *Duncan* **Pigment ink:** (Seafoam) *Tsukineko* **Accents:** (fabric label) *Making Memories*; (mini shells) *Limited Edition Rubberstamps* **Fibers:** (mesh ribbon)

MAKES ONE 4¼" x 8¼" CARD

## Outstanding Performance

Designer: Sande Krieger

SUPPLIES
**Patterned paper:** (BW Thin Stripe from Black on Worn collection) *Scenic Route Paper Co.* **Paper accent:** (A+ Achieve coaster) *Cloud 9 Design*; (manila tag) *Office Depot* **Accents:** (decorative brad) *Crafts, Etc.* **Rub-ons:** (sentiment) *Making Memories* **Fibers:** (white diamond ribbon) *May Arts*

MAKES ONE 3½" x 5" CARD

**TIP A LA SANDE**
*Create a pocket instead of a flap for an innovative variation on the recipe.*

## Love Times Three

Designer: Wendy Johnson

### SUPPLIES

**Textured cardstock:** (Raven) *Bazzill Basics Paper* **Patterned paper:** (Cinnamon Rustic Gingham) *Paper Patch* **Paper accents:** (square metal-rimmed tags) *Making Memories* **Accent:** (Love charm) *Creative Imaginations* **Fibers:** (¾" and ¼" black gingham ribbons) *Offray* **Adhesive:** (foam tape) *3M;* (glue stick) **Tools:** (Folk Heart punch, square punch) Paper Shapers, *EK Success;* (scissors, craft knife, hole punch)

MAKES ONE 5" x 7" CARD

*This trio of windows offers unlimited creativity potential. Use photos, accents, charms, sentiments, and more for a classy and unique design.*

### INSTRUCTIONS

❶ Cut cardstock to 10" x 7". ❷ Score and fold in half. ❸ Cut three windows along right edge with craft knife or square punch. ❹ Use windows as canvas for embellishments.

### INSTRUCTIONS

❶ Make card from Raven cardstock, following instructions at left. ❷ Cut Cinnamon Rustic Gingham paper to fit card front; adhere and trim to show windows. ❸ Trim punched Raven scraps to fit tags; adhere. ❹ Punch Folk Heart three times from Cinnamon Rustic Gingham and adhere to tags with foam tape. ❺ Punch holes in tags and in card above each window; thread ribbons through holes and tie knots to secure. ❻ Attach ribbon and charm to card.

## Simply Missing You

Designer: Wendy Sue Anderson

SUPPLIES

**Textured cardstock:** (Wheat) *Bazzill Basics Paper*
**Patterned paper:** (Life's Journey Script, Floral)
*K&Company*; (Weathered 327) *Paper Loft* **Dye**
**ink:** (Sand) Memories, *Stewart Superior Corp.*
**Accents:** (leather flower) *Making Memories*;
(mesh) **Rub-ons:** (i, miss, you) Simply Stated,
*Making Memories* **Fasteners:** (button eyelets)
*K&Company*; (silver brad) *Making Memories*
**Fibers:** (raffia) **Adhesive:** (glue stick) **Tools:**
scissors, eyelet-setting tools, craft knife

MAKES ONE 5" x 7" CARD

## Seasonal Trio

Designer: Lori Allred

SUPPLIES

**Textured cardstock:** (Crimson) *Bazzill Basics Paper*
**Acrylic paint:** (Spotlight) Cityscape, Scrapbook
Colors, *Making Memories* **Accents:** (Diamond)
Metal Mesh, (present, tree, stocking) Charmed,
*Making Memories* **Fibers:** (green gingham, red
gingham ribbons) *Making Memories* **Font:** (2Ps
Submarine) www.twopeasinabucket.com **Adhesive:**
(metal adhesive, dots) **Tools:** scissors, craft
knife, paintbrush, computer and printer

MAKES ONE 5" x 7" CARD

### SECRET INGREDIENTS

*To create text around windows, experiment with
Word Art on a blank sheet of paper before printing
on cardstock. Or simply stamp sentiments with
your favorite alphabet set.*

## Flower Boxes

Designer: Marla Bird

SUPPLIES

**Textured cardstock:** (Navy) *Pebbles Inc.*
**Patterned paper:** (Den Paisley) Den Collection,
*Chatterbox* **Accents:** (wire flowers) Eco Africa,
*Provo Craft* **Adhesive:** (craft glue) Aleene's
Original Tacky Glue, *Duncan* **Tools:** scissors,
craft knife, bone folder

MAKES ONE 5" x 7" CARD

## Our Neck of the Woods

Designer: Wendy Johnson

### SUPPLIES

**Cardstock:** (white, kraft) **Textured cardstock:** (Buttercream) *Bazzill Basics Paper* **Patterned paper:** (Grad Plaid, Into the Woods) *Karen Foster Design* **Color medium:** (brown chalk) *Craf-T Products* **Accents:** (wooden skewer, black wire) **Fibers:** (red gingham ribbon) *Making Memories* **Font:** (Chestnuts) *www.twopeasinabucket.com* **Adhesive:** foam squares

MAKES ONE 4¾" x 5¾" CARD

### INSTRUCTIONS

❶ Make 5" x 5½" white card. Using the recipe as a template, trace tree shape on card with fold at top; cut out. *Note: Leave ½" fold at top instead of tree point.* ❷ Cut moon shape from Buttercream cardstock; chalk edges and attach to card with wire. ❸ Trace template on Into the Woods paper; cut out and adhere to card. ❹ Cut triangle of kraft cardstock; chalk edges. Cut slit and fold back flaps for tent. ❺ Cut triangle of Grad Plaid paper; adhere behind tent. Adhere tent to card with foam squares. ❻ Print "Welcome to our neck of the woods!" on white; mat with kraft. Trim border of mat and chalk edges. Adhere sign to skewer; knot ribbon and adhere skewer to card. ❼ Print family name on white, chalk edges, and adhere to tent.

## Simple Snowman

Designer: Heather D. White

SUPPLIES

**Textured cardstock:** (White, Black, Orange) *Die Cuts With a View* **Dye ink:** (Black) *Plaid* **Fibers:** (red ribbon) *Making Memories*

MAKES ONE 3⅝" x 4¾" CARD

### TIP A LA HEATHER

*Don't let familiar shapes limit your creativity. Allow your imagination to take flight and create fun new designs from tried-and-true ideas.*

## Merry Little Christmas

Designer: Susan Neal

SUPPLIES

**Cardstock:** (Stonehenge) *Bazzill Basics Paper* **Patterned paper:** (Christmas Quilt) *Daisy D's* **Rubber stamps:** (Merry Little Christmas) *Inkadinkado;* (flourish from Fancy Flourishes

set) *Hero Arts* **Pigment ink:** (Vintage Sepia, Onyx Black) *Tsukineko* **Accents:** (pewter photo turns, pewter mini brads) *Making Memories* **Fibers:** (red cord) *Making Memories* **Adhesive:** (foam squares) *Therm O Web* **Die:** (Primitive Star) *Provo Craft/Ellison*

MAKES ONE 4" x 5¼" CARD

### TIP A LA SUSAN

*Adapt the recipe to make an interactive card from a flat design. Susan added a lift-up flap that reveals a message of holiday cheer.*

INSIDE

## Summer Camp Album

Designer: Dee Gallimore-Perry

SUPPLIES

**Cardstock:** (White) *Bazzill Basics Paper* **Patterned paper:** (green plaid from Cousins collection) *My Mind's Eye* **Paper accents:** (children die cuts) *My Mind's Eye* **Fibers:** (green polka dot ribbon) *Offray* **Font:** (Kids) www.momscorner4kids.com

MAKES ONE 5" x 5¾" CARD

### TIP A LA DEE

*Make a mini album by attaching pages to the embellished cover. Kids can take this to camp for autographs or personal messages from the friends they meet there. After their return, you can also include this in a scrapbooking layout with photos of all the camping highlights.*

## Birthday Boy Tag

Designer: Wendy Johnson

### SUPPLIES

**Cardstock:** (white) **Textured cardstock:** (Orange Crush) *Bazzill Basics Paper* **Patterned paper:** (Seth Multi Checkered Plaid) *Treehouse Memories* **Paper accent:** (sentiment) *Treehouse Memories* **Accent:** (blue brad) *Making Memories;* (key) **Fibers:** (twill ribbon) **Font:** (Quirky) *www.twopeasinabucket.com* **Tools:** (circle cutter) *Creative Memories*

MAKES ONE 5¼" DIAMETER CARD

### INSTRUCTIONS

① Cut circle of patterned paper; mat with Orange Crush cardstock. ② Adhere sentiment to tag. ③ Adhere loop of twill ribbon to card for tab. ④ Print "Sweet 16" on white cardstock; trim and mat with Orange Crush. ⑤ Attach printed sentiment and key to tag with brad.

### TIP A LA WENDY

*Make tags exciting again with new shapes and sizes. This big, round tag will enhance any birthday gift. You can even forgo a card and write your happy wishes on the back of the tag.*

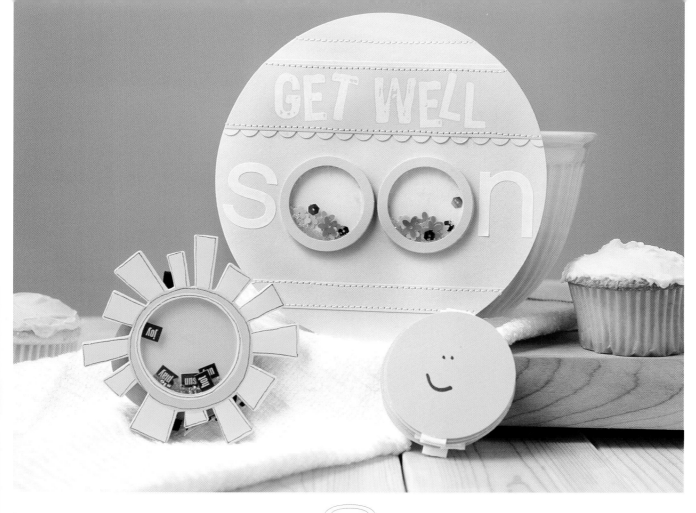

## You Are My Sunshine

Designer: Marla Bird

**SUPPLIES**

**Sunshine shaker box:** *Provo Craft* **Cardstock:**
(white) **Textured cardstock:** (yellow) **Dye ink:**
(black) **Accents:** (black photo turn, paper clip)
*7gypsies*; (black brad, bead chain) *Pebbles
Inc.* **Fibers:** (black and white, black ribbon)
*Making Memories* **Font:** (Butterbrotpapier)
*www.momscorner4kids.com* **Tools:** circle punch

MAKES ONE 3½" x 11½" CARD

### TIP A LA MARLA

*Print the sentiment in reverse type on white
cardstock for a cool yellow-on-black effect.*

You

are my

Sunshine

INSIDE

---

### APPETIZING IDEA

*This sunny greeting is just one of the ways you can
interpret this recipe. Think of other round shapes with
drop-down elements that recipients would love: a
flower with leaves, a bunch of balloons, a beach ball
with sand toys, sports balls—the possibilities are endless.*

## Get Well Soon Shaker

Designer: Nichole Heady

**SUPPLIES**

**Cardstock:** (Turquoise) *Close To My Heart*; (Soft
Green, Soft Blue from Baby Boy collection) *Deja
Views* **Transparency sheet; Accents:** (tiny glass
beads) *Stampin' Up!*; (flower sequins) *Willow
Bead* **Rub-ons:** (alphabet) **Stickers:** (Runway
alphabet) *American Crafts* **Fibers:** (white thread)
**Tools:** (1¾", 1⅜" circle punches) *EK Success*;
(decorative-edge scissors) *Stampin' Up!*

MAKES ONE 6" DIAMETER CARD

### TIP A LA NICHOLE

*Create a sturdy shaker box by punching nine
cardstock circles. Then, punch each circle
with a smaller circle to create a ring.
Stack them together, adhering each layer.
Adhere the top ring to the transparency sheet.*

---

## Miles of Smiles

Designer: Sara Horton

**SUPPLIES**

**Cardstock:** (white) **Textured cardstock:** (Yellow) *Die
Cuts With a View* **Color medium:** (black marker) **Font:**
(Pharmacy) *www.dafont.com* **Tools:** circle punch

MAKES ONE 2¼" DIAMETER CLOSED CARD
OPEN 31" x 2¼"

### TIP A LA SARA

*Connect the smiley circles in this project
with a thin strip cut from cardstock. You don't
have to be limited to any length, because you can
adhere two strips together for a longer chain.*

wishing you
miles of smiles on
your birthday!

INSIDE

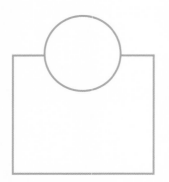

## Live Out Loud

Designer: Wendy Sue Anderson

SUPPLIES
**Cardstock:** (lime green) **Patterned paper:**
(Girl Floral) *Junkitz* **Dye ink:** (Black) *Stewart
Superior Corp.*; (red) **Rub-ons:** (sentiment)
*Deja Views* **Fibers:** (green gingham, green and
red dotted ribbon) **Tools:** circle cutter

MAKES ONE 5" x 6" CARD

INSTRUCTIONS
1 Make card from patterned paper;
lay flat and cut half circle along fold.
2 Cut circle from lime green cardstock;
ink edges with Black and adhere to card
(see photo). 3 Apply rub-on. *Note: Apply
exclamation point inside card to line
up with sentiment when card is open.*
4 Cut strip of lime green; ink with Black
and red. Adhere to card. 5 Tie ribbon
around card front; knot.

## Big Button Birthday

Designer: Wendy Johnson

SUPPLIES
**Cardstock:** (Green Tea Solid) *KI Memories*;
(white) **Patterned paper:** (Starry Starry Night from
Evergreen collection) *KI Memories* **Accent:** (green
button) *Blumenthal Lansing Co.* **Fibers:** (lavender
stitched ribbon) *Michaels* **Font:** (Flower Pot)
*www.twopeasinabucket.com*

MAKES ONE 3¾" x 4¼" CARD

### TIP A LA WENDY
*Vary the recipe by using a round focal point on a
tent-fold card instead of an insert. The big button
on this card is a fun twist on the original idea.*

## No Pain, No Gain

Designer: Alice Golden

SUPPLIES
**Cardstock:** (Pool Water Blue from Swimsuit
Edition collection) *Arctic Frog* **Patterned paper:**
(Suspenders from Grandpa's Attic collection) *SEI*;
(Type Count) *Rusty Pickle* **Dye ink:** (Black Soot)
*Ranger Industries* **Accents:** (ribbon slide, round
metal sign) *Making Memories*; (mini screw brads)
*Karen Foster Design* **Rub-ons:** (sentiments)
*Making Memories* **Stickers:** (sports phrases)
*Karen Foster Design* **Fibers:** (leather trim) *Karen
Foster Design* **Tools:** circle punch

MAKES ONE 4" x 5¼" CARD

### TIP A LA ALICE
*Give this unique card to someone
with a weight-training or weight-loss goal, a
runner who's finished a marathon, or your
favorite athlete after the big game.*

### SPICE IT UP
*Ensure that your good wishes will be remembered
by making the metal sign on this card into a
detachable refrigerator magnet. Simply adhere the
sign to an adhesive-backed magnet sheet, trim,
and place on the insert with double-sided tape.*

INSIDE

## Special Delivery

Designer: Susan Neal

SUPPLIES
**Cardstock:** (Black, Stonehenge) *Bazzill Basics
Paper* **Textured cardstock:** (Blossom, Light Olive)
*Bazzill Basics Paper* **Patterned paper:** (English
Floral) *K&Company* **Rubber stamp:** (Special
Delivery; quote from Sentiments set) *Inkadinkado*
**Pigment ink:** (Vintage Sepia, Onyx Black) *Tsukineko*
**Fibers:** (olive sheer ribbon) *Making Memories*
**Adhesive:** foam squares **Tools:** circle punch

MAKES ONE 4⅛" x 5" CARD

### TIP A LA SUSAN
*Write a personal note to the recipient on
the insert. Or, use this card as an invitation and
print event details on the insert card.*

INSIDE

205

## B Is for Baby

Designer: Susan Neal

### SUPPLIES

**Textured cardstock:** (Cameo, Cornbread) *Bazzill Basics Paper* **Patterned paper:** (Baby Script Blush, Baby Script Buttercream) *Daisy D's* **Rubber stamps:** (Baby) *DeNami Design*; (Baby Blessings) *Hero Arts*; (Yippie!) *Wordsworth*; (Antique UC Alphabet, Antique LC Alphabet) *Duncan*; (angel from Baby set) *7gypsies* **Dye ink:** (Tea Dye) *Ranger Industries* **Pigment ink:** (Onyx Black) *Tsukineko* **Color medium:** (black fine-point marker) **Paint:** (Oyster White) *Delta* **Paper accents:** (cardboard letters) *Making Memories* **Accents:** (silver brad) *American Crafts*; (acrylic flowers) *Maya Road* **Fibers:** (yellow and black ribbon) *Making Memories*; (white rickrack) *Wrights*; (pink ribbon, fibers) **Dies:** (oval tag) *Provo Craft/Ellison*

MAKES ONE 2½" x 4" CARD

### INSTRUCTIONS

❶ Punch two ovals from Cameo cardstock and two ovals from Cornbread cardstock; ink edges with Tea Dye. ❷ Adhere patterned paper to ovals as desired; ink edges. ❸ Apply paint to cardboard letters; let dry and sand edges. *Note: Apply two coats for best coverage.* ❹ Embellish each tag with ribbon, cardboard letters, accents, and sentiments. ❺ Secure tags together at top with brad.

### SECRET INGREDIENTS

*The Baby Blessings stamp from Hero Arts has been discontinued and may be difficult to find. Instead, use alphabet stamps to create exactly the sentiment you desire.*

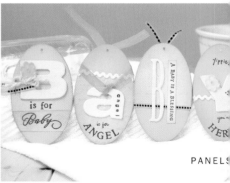

PANELS

## Love You

Designer: Wendy Sue Anderson

SUPPLIES
*All supplies from Making Memories unless otherwise noted.*

**Patterned paper:** (Wild Cherry, Green Apple, Pink Lemonade from Lollipop Shoppe collection) *BasicGrey* **Paint:** (Spotlight) **Paper accents:** (love tags); (Rainbow Sorbet tag) *BasicGrey* **Accent:** (metal heart plaque) **Rub-ons:** (sentiments) **Fibers:** (assorted red ribbon, printed black ribbon)

MAKES ONE 2¼" x 3½" CARD

### TIP A LA WENDY SUE

*This project is a great way to use up all those paper and accent scraps you have lying around.*

## Forever Promise

Designer: Michelle Tardie

SUPPLIES
**Textured cardstock:** (Princess) *Bazzill Basics Paper* **Paper accents:** (sentiment die cut) *We R Memory Keepers* **Accents:** (pink brads) *All My Memories* **Stickers:** (phrase labels) *K&Company* **Fibers:** (pink rickrack) *EK Success*

MAKES ONE 5¾" x 3¾" CARD

### TIP A LA MICHELLE

*Create an oval card by cutting two matching ovals from cardstock. Punch two holes on one edge, and tie together with rickrack. Michelle added a brad in each hole on the front oval for a fancier look.*

## Graduation Success

Designer: Wendy Johnson

SUPPLIES
**Cardstock:** (Cream) *Provo Craft* **Textured cardstock:** (Parakeet) *Bazzill Basics Paper* **Patterned paper:** (Birthday Stripe Classic Blue) *Daisy D's* **Accents:** (silver brads) *Creative Imaginations*; (blue brads) *Making Memories* **Rub-ons:** (sentiment) *My Mind's Eye*

MAKES ONE 6¾" x 5" CARD

INSIDE

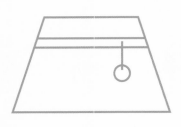

a

MAKE MARK ½" IN ON EDGES; TRIM
DIAGONALLY TO BOTTOM FOLD.

*This unique trapezoidal card can be customized for
any occasion. Use it as a base for creative items like
a purse, or simply embellish to your liking.*

## INSTRUCTIONS

❶ Cut cardstock to 6" x 10". ❷ Score
and fold in half. ❸ Trim top corners away
as shown (see Figure a). ❹ Embellish
as desired.

## Celebrate...

Designer: Wendy Johnson

### SUPPLIES

**Cardstock:** (bright pink) **Textured cardstock:** (Limeade) *Bazzill Basics Paper* **Patterned paper:**
(Sisters Pink) *American Crafts* **Paper accent:** (round metal-rimmed tag) *Avery Dennison* **Accents:**
(pink spiral clips) *Impress Rubber Stamps*; (green buttons) Dress It Up, *Jesse James & Co.* **Rub-
ons:** (Celebrate) Simply Stated. *Making Memories* **Fibers:** (green and pink ribbon) *May Arts*; (white
floss) *DMC* **Adhesive:** (glue stick) **Tools:** (circle punch) Paper Shapers, *EK Success*; (scissors)
MAKES ONE 6" x 5" CARD

### INSTRUCTIONS

❶ Make card from Limeade cardstock,
following instructions at left. ❷ Cut
sisters Pink paper to fit bottom two-thirds
of card front; trim and adhere. ❸ Punch
circle of bright pink cardstock; adhere to
tag. ❹ Adhere buttons to tag; thread floss
and tie around ribbon. ❺ Adhere ribbon
over seam between papers. ❻ Apply
rub-on and attach clips at top.

## Polka-Dot Purse

Designer: Marla Bird

SUPPLIES
**Cardstock:** (Cream) *Pebbles Inc.* **Textured cardstock:** (Petunia) *Bazzill Basics Paper* **Patterned paper:** (brown/cream polka dot) **Accents:** (cream buttons) *Dress It Up, Jesse James & Co.*; (craft foam) **Adhesive:** (craft glue) *Aleene's Original Tacky Glue, Duncan* **Tools:** (Doodlebug Alphabar "S", die-cut machine) *Provo Craft/Ellison*; (scissors)
MAKES ONE 6" x 5" CARD

**APPETIZING IDEA**
*For a unique variation, die-cut from leather, metal or shrink plastic. Personalize the card with the recipient's initials.*

## Get Well Soon

Designer: Sande Krieger

SUPPLIES
**Cardstock:** (dark brown) **Patterned paper:** (Stucco Motif) *BasicGrey* **Rubber stamp:** (Get Well Soon) *Hero Arts* **Dye ink:** (Basic Black) Classic Stampin' Pad, *Stampin' Up!* **Paper accent:** (Motifica tag) *BasicGrey* **Fasteners:** (antique brads) *Creative Impressions*; (triangle clip) *The Weathered Door* **Fibers:** (twill ribbon) *Scenic Route Paper Co.*; (brown floss) *Waxy Flax, Scrapworks* **Adhesive:** (glue stick) **Tools:** scissors, bone folder
MAKES ONE 6" x 5" CARD

## Father's Overalls

Designer: Nichole Heady

SUPPLIES
**Cardstock:** (Night of Navy) *Stampin' Up!* **Accents:** (green buttons) *SEI*; (Je T'aime label from Love set) SC Threads, *Me & My Big Ideas* **Stickers:** (Garden Shed Green alphabet) *All My Memories*; (green alphabet) *LizKing, EK Success* **Fibers:** (Navy ribbon) *Stampin' Up!*; (white floss) *DMC* **Adhesive:** (dots) *Glue Dots International*; (glue stick) **Tools:** scissors, needle
MAKES ONE 6" x 5" CARD

**APPETIZING IDEAS**
*Adapt this card for a personalized look for any recipient: make it into a jumper for a little girl, or use denim patterned paper and tool charms.*

## Flower Pot Greeting

Designer: Wendy Johnson

SUPPLIES

**Cardstock:** (white) **Textured cardstock:** (Green Tea, Powder, Pinata, Kraft, Lemonade OP) *Bazzill Basics Paper* **Patterned paper:** (Maple Sugar/Vanilla from Homespun collection) *Bo-Bunny Press* **Color medium:** (brown chalk) *Craf-T Products* **Accents:** (blue brad) *The Happy Hammer;* (wooden skewers) **Fibers:** (olive grosgrain ribbon) *Die Cuts With a View* **Font:** (Evergreen) *www.twopeasinabucket.com* **Adhesive:** foam squares *3M* **Tools:** circle, flower punch

MAKES ONE 4" X 8" CARD

### CARD

❶ Cut 9" x 3¾" rectangle of Kraft cardstock. Fold in half and trim into flower pot shape; chalk edges. *Note: Fold should be at bottom.* ❷ Cut Maple Sugar/Vanilla paper to fit card front; adhere ribbon. Adhere piece to card. ❸ Cut strip of Maple Sugar/Vanilla; trim one edge into scallops, chalk edges, and adhere to card with foam squares. ❹ Print "For you" on white cardstock; trim into tag shape, mat with Pinata cardstock, and attach to card with brad.

### INSIDE

❶ Punch two flowers each from Green Tea, Powder, and Pinata cardstock; adhere same color flowers to varying lengths of skewers. ❷ Punch three circles from Lemonade OP cardstock; chalk edges and adhere to flowers with foam squares. ❸ Adhere flower sticks inside card. ❹ Print "Bloom where you are planted!" on Kraft cardstock; chalk edges and trim to fit inside card. Adhere over skewers with foam squares.

INSIDE

## Just Because

Designer: JoAnne Bacon

SUPPLIES
**Cardstock:** (white) **Patterned paper:** (Spring Stars, Green Field from Flutter collection) *Autumn Leaves* **Accent:** (acrylic sentiment) *KI Memories* **Fibers:** (pink striped ribbon) *KI Memories*

MAKES ONE 4" x 6¾" CARD

## For a Speedy Recovery

Designer: Kathleen Paneitz

SUPPLIES
**Cardstock:** (white) **Textured cardstock:** (Yellow) *Die Cuts With a View* **Patterned paper:** (Red & Cream Gingham) *Rusty Pickle* **Rubber stamps:** (script alphabet) *Crafty Secrets* **Accent:** (photo turn) *7gypsies*; (silver washer eyelet) *Creative Impressions* **Rub-ons:** (black stitching) *My Mind's Eye* **Stickers:** (Tiny Alphabet Small) *Making Memories* **Fibers:** (black gingham ribbon) *Offray* **Other:** sandpaper

MAKES ONE 3¾" x 4¾" CARD

## Baby Be Mine Gift Bag

Designer: Alisa Bangerter

SUPPLIES
**Patterned paper:** (Love Notes, Candy Confessions from Crush collection) *Scrapworks* **Paint:** (pink, fuchsia) **Accents:** (acrylic hearts) *Heidi Swapp*; (plastic buckle) *Junkitz* **Tools:** (decorative-edge scissors) *Fiskars*

MAKES ONE 4" x 6" x 2" BAG

*Note: Gift bag pattern on p. 212*

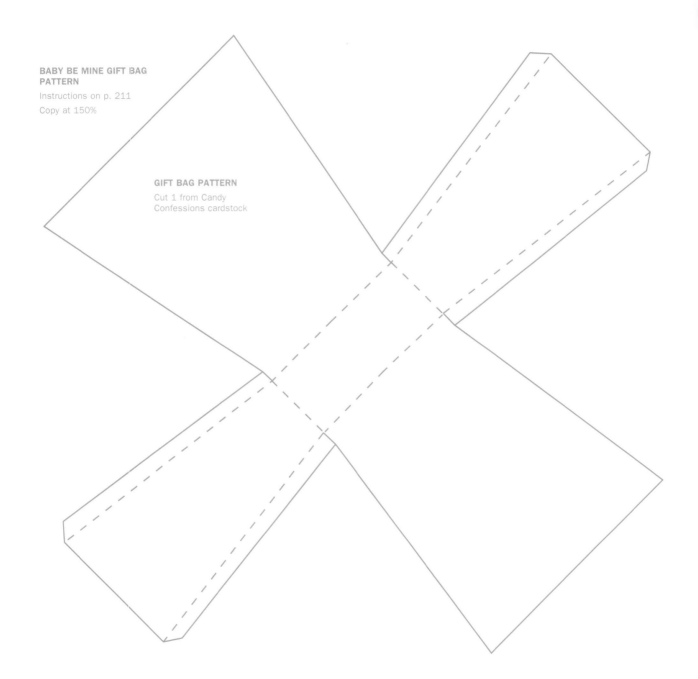

**BABY BE MINE GIFT BAG PATTERN**
Instructions on p. 211
Copy at 150%

**GIFT BAG PATTERN**
Cut 1 from Candy
Confessions cardstock

# Product Guide

The following information is for supplies used in this issue's projects. Check for them at your local craft store or retail chain. Be sure to enter *www.* before each Web site address.

ACCENT DEPOT
630/548-2133
*accentdepot.com*

ACE HARDWARE
866/290-5334
*acehardware.com*

ADOBE SYSTEMS INCORPORATED
888/724-4508
*adobe.com*

ALL MY MEMORIES
801/572-9199
*allmymemories.com*

AMERICAN CRAFTS
800/879-5185
*americancrafts.com*

AMERICAN GREETINGS
*americangreetings.com*

AMERICAN LABEL & TAG CO.
313/626-6614

AMERICAN TRADITIONAL DESIGNS
800/278-3624
*americantraditional.com*

ANNA GRIFFIN INC.
888/817-8170
*annagriffin.com*

ANGEL COMPANY, THE
785/820-9181
*theangelcompany.net*

ARCTIC FROG
479/636-FROG
*arcticfrog.net*

ARTISTIC WIRE
800/245-9473
*artisticwire.com*

AUTUMN LEAVES
800/588-6707
*autumnleaves.com*

AVERY DENNISON CORPORATION
800/GO-AVERY
*avery.com*

BASICGREY
801/451-6006
*basicgrey.com*

BAZZILL BASICS PAPER
480/558-8557
*bazzillbasics.com*

BO-BUNNY PRESS
801/771-4010
*bobunny.com*

BOUTIQUE TRIMS
248/437-2017
*boutiquetrims.com*

BLUMENTHAL LANSING COMPANY
563/538-4211
*buttonsplus.com*

BUTTONS GALORE & MORE
856/753-6700
*buttonsgaloreandmore.com*

CAROLEE'S CREATIONS
435/563-1100
*caroleescreations.com*

CHATTERBOX, INC.
888/416-6260
*chatterboxinc.com*

CLEARSNAP, INC.
800/448-4862
*clearsnap.com*

C-LINE PRODUCTS
800/323-6084
*c-lineproducts.com*

CLOUD 9 DESIGN
763/493-0990
*cloud9design.biz*

CLOSE TO MY HEART
*closetomyheart.com*

COREL
800/772-6735
*corel.com*

CRAFT PEDLARS, THE
*pedlars.com*

CRAF-T PRODUCTS
*craf-tproducts.com*

CRAFTS, ETC.
800/888-0321
*craftsetc.com*

CREATE-A-CRAFT
Available at Wal-Mart

CREATING KEEPSAKES MAGAZINE
888/247-5282
*creatingkeepsakes.com*

CREATIVE IMAGINATIONS
800/942-6487
*cigift.com*

CREATIVE IMPRESSIONS
719/577-4858
*creativeimpressions.com*

CREEK BANK CREATIONS
217/427-5980
*creekbankcreations.com*

C-THRU RULER COMPANY
800/243-8419
*cthruruler.com*

DAISY D'S PAPER CO.
888/601-8955
*daisydotsanddoodles.com*

DARICE
800/321-1494
*darice.com*

DCC CRAFTS
800/835-3013
*dcccrafts.com*

DELUXE DESIGNS
480/497-9005
*deluxecuts.com*

DELUXE PLASTIC ARTS, (in India)
91-22-4973525

DERWENT CUMBERLAND PENCIL CO.
*pencils.co.uk*

DMC
973/589-0606
*dmc-usa.com*

DMD, INC.
800/805-9890
*dmdind.com*

DOLPHIN ENTERPRISES
877/910-3360
*protect-a-page.com*

DOODLEBUG DESIGN INC.
*doodlebugdesigninc.com*

DOVE BRUSHES
*dovebrushes.com*

DUNCAN ENTERPRISES
800/438-6226
*duncancrafts.com*

DYMO
800/426-7827
*dymo.com*

ECLECTIC PRODUCTS, INC.
800/693-4667
*eclecticproducts.com*

EK SUCCESS
800/767-2963
*eksuccess.com*

EMAGINATION CRAFTS INC.
866/238-9770
*emaginationcrafts.com*

ELLISON
800/253-2238
*ellison.com*

FAMILY TREASURES
949/643-9526
*familytreasures.com*

FISKARS
800/950-0203
*fiskars.com*

FOOFALA
402/330-3208
*foofala.com*

FROST CREEK CHARMS
763/684-0074
*frostcreekcharms.com*

GARTNER STUDIOS, INC.
*uprint.com*

GLUE DOTS INTERNATIONAL
*gluedots.com*

GONE SCRAPPIN'
435/647-0404
*gonescrappin.com*

GO WEST STUDIOS
214/227-0007
*goweststudios.com*

HAMMERMILL
800/242-2148
*hammermill.com*

HAPPY HAMMER, THE
*thehappyhammer.com*

HEARTLAND PAPER CO.
801/294-7166
*heartlandpaper.com*

HEIDI GRACE DESIGNS
866/89-HEIDI
*heidigrace.com*

HERO ARTS
800/822-HERO
*heroarts.com*

HIRSCHBERG SCHUTZ & CO.
800/543-5442

HOT OFF THE PRESS
888/300-3406
*craftpizazz.com*

HYGLO CRAFTS
480/968-6475
*hyglocrafts.com*

IMPRESS RUBBER STAMPS
206/901-9101
*impressrubberstamps.com*

INKADINKADO
800/888-4652
*inkadinkado.com*

IT TAKES TWO
800/967-3365
*ittakestwo.com*

JESSE JAMES & CO. INC.
*dressitup.com*

JKM RIBBON (MOREX CORP.)
717/852-7771, ext. 238
jkmribbon.com

JO-ANN STORES
888/739-4120
joann.com

JONES TONES, INC.
719/948-0048
jonestones.com

JUNKITZ
732/792-1108
junkitz.com

K&COMPANY
888/244-2083
kandcompany.com

KANGAROO AND JOEY
480/460-4841
kangarooandjoey.com

KAREN FOSTER DESIGN
scrapbookpaper.com

KEEPING MEMORIES ALIVE
800/419-4949
scrapbooks.com

KI MEMORIES
469/633-9665
kimemories.com

KOPP DESIGN
801/489-6011
koppdesign.com

KRYLON
800/457-9566
krylon.com

LASTING IMPRESSIONS FOR PAPER
800/9-EMBOSS
lastingimpressions.com

LIFETIME MOMENTS
760/806-7788
lifetimemoments.com

LI'L DAVIS DESIGNS
949/838-0344
lildavisdesigns.com

LIMITED EDITION RUBBERSTAMPS
877/9-STAMPS
limitededitionrs.com

LUCKY SQUIRREL
800/462-4912
luckysquirrel.com

MAGENTA RUBBER STAMPS
magentarubberstamps.com

MAGIC SCRAPS
972/238-1838
magicscraps.com

MAKING MEMORIES
801/294-0430
makingmemories.com

MARCEL SCHURMAN
schurmanfinepapers.com

MA VINCI'S RELIQUARY
crafts.dm.net/mall/reliquary

MARVY UCHIDA
800/541-5877
uchida.com

MAUDE AND MILLIE
763/639-9615
maudeandmillie.com

MAY ARTS
800/442-3950

MCGILL, INC.
800/982-9884
mcgillinc.com

ME & MY BIG IDEAS
949/583-2065
meandmybigideas.com

MEMORIES COMPLETE
866/966.6365
memoriescomplete.com

MEMORY LANE PAPER COMPANY
801/226-1159
memorylanepaper.com

MICHAELS STORES, INC.
800/642-4235
michaels.com

MICROSOFT
800/936-5700
microsoft.com

MPR PAPERBILITIES
available through scrpbkfanatic.com

MRS. GROSSMAN'S
800/429-4549
mrsgrossmans.com

MY MIND'S EYE
800/665-5116
frame-ups.com

NATIONAL CARDSTOCK
866/452-7120
nationalcardstock.com

NICOLE INDUSTRIES
sbarsonline.com

NRN DESIGNS
nrndesigns.com

NSI INNOVATIONS
888/425-9113
nsiinnovations.com

OFFICEMAX
800/283-7674
officemax.com

OFFRAY
800/237-9425
offray.com

O'SCRAP!
801/225-6015
imaginations-inc.com

PAPER DAISY SCRAPBOOK CO.
801/356-1866

PAPERFEVER
800/477-0902
paperfever.com

PAPER LADY, THE
888/355-1418
thepaperladyinc.com

PAPER LOFT
801/254-1961
paperloft.com

PAPER PATCH, THE
paperpatch.com

PATCHWORK PAPER DESIGN, INC.
480/515-0537
patchworkpaper.com

PEBBLES INC.
800/235-1520
pebblesinc.com

PEBBLES IN MY POCKET
800/438-8153
pebblesinmypocket.com

PIONEER PHOTO ALBUMS, INC.
818/882-2161
pioneerphotoalbums.com

PLAID ENTERPRISES, INC.
800/842-4197
plaidonline.com

PM DESIGNS
888/595-2887
puzzlemates.com

PRESSED PETALS
pressedpetals.com

PRINTWORKS
800/854-6558
printworkscollection.com

PROVO CRAFT
800/937-7686
provocraft.com

PRYM-DRITZ CORPORATION
dritz.com

RANGER INDUSTRIES
800/244-2211
rangerink.com

ROBIN'S NEST, THE
435/789-5387

RUSTY PICKLE
801/746-1045
rustypickle.com

SANDYLION STICKER DESIGNS
800/387-4215
sandylion.com

SANFORD CORP.
800/323-0749
sanfordcorp.com

SAVVY STAMPS
360/833-4555
savvystamps.com

SCENIC ROUTE PAPER CO.
801/785-0761
scenicroutepaper.com

SCRAPARTS
503/631-4893
scraparts.com

SCRAP PAGERZ
435/647-0404
scrappagerz.co

SCRAPWORKS, LLC
scrapworks.com

SCRAPYARD 329
scrapyard329.com

SEI
800/333-3279
shopsei.com

7GYPSIES
800/588-6707
7gypsies.com

STAMPABILITIES
800/888-0321
stampabilities.com

STAMPIN' UP!
800/STAMP UP
stampinup.com

STEWART SUPERIOR CORPORATION
800/558-2875
stewartsuperior.com

SUE DREAMER
suedreamer.com

SWEETWATER
970/867-4428
sweetwaterscrapbook.com

TARGET
888/440-0680
target.com

3M (ADHESIVES DIVISION)
800/364-3577
3m.com

TSUKINEKO
800/769-6633
tsukineko.com

TUMBLEBEASTS
505/323-5554

TURTLE PRESS
turtlearts.com

TWO PEAS IN A BUCKET
twopeasinabucket.com

WIMPOLE STREET CREATIONS
(BARRETT HOUSE)
800/432-5776
barrett-house.com

WEATHERED DOOR, THE
253/227-9219
theweathereddoor.com

WE R MEMORY KEEPERS
877/PICK WE R
weronthenet.com

WESTRIM CRAFTS
800/727-2727
westrimcrafts.com

WOOHOO WOWIES
Available at scrapbookinglife.com.au

WRIGHTS
888/394-3576
wrights.com

XYRON
800/793-3523
xyron.com

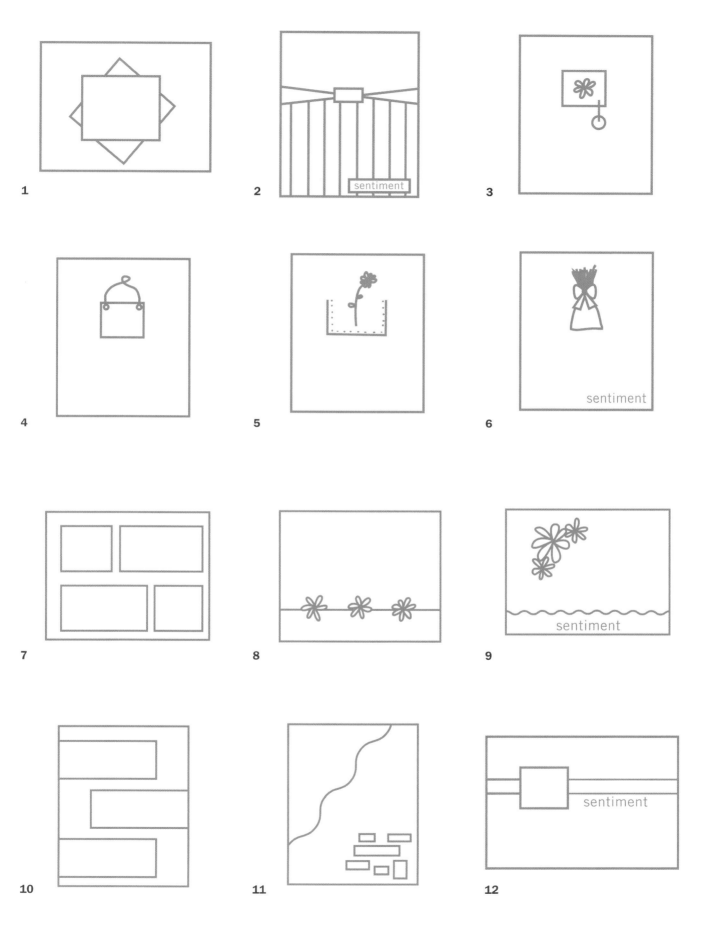

1

2

sentiment

3

4

5

6

sentiment

7

8

9

sentiment

10

11

12

sentiment

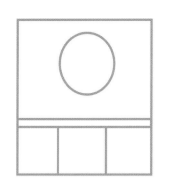

**13**

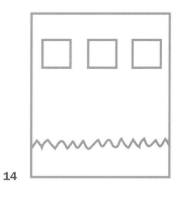

**14**

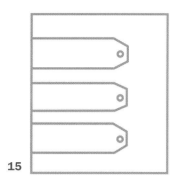

**15**

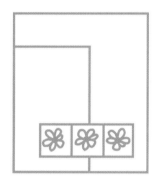

**16**

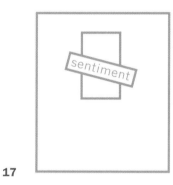

sentiment

**17**

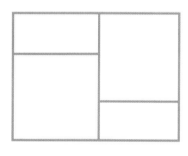

**18**

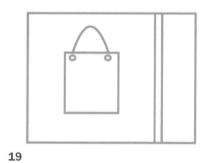

**19**

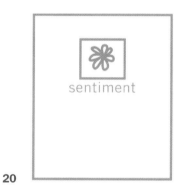

sentiment

**20**

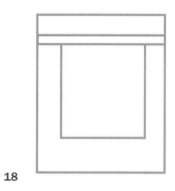

**21**

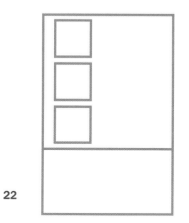

**22**

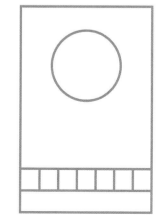

**23**

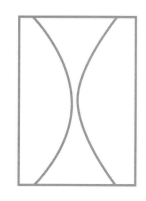

**24**

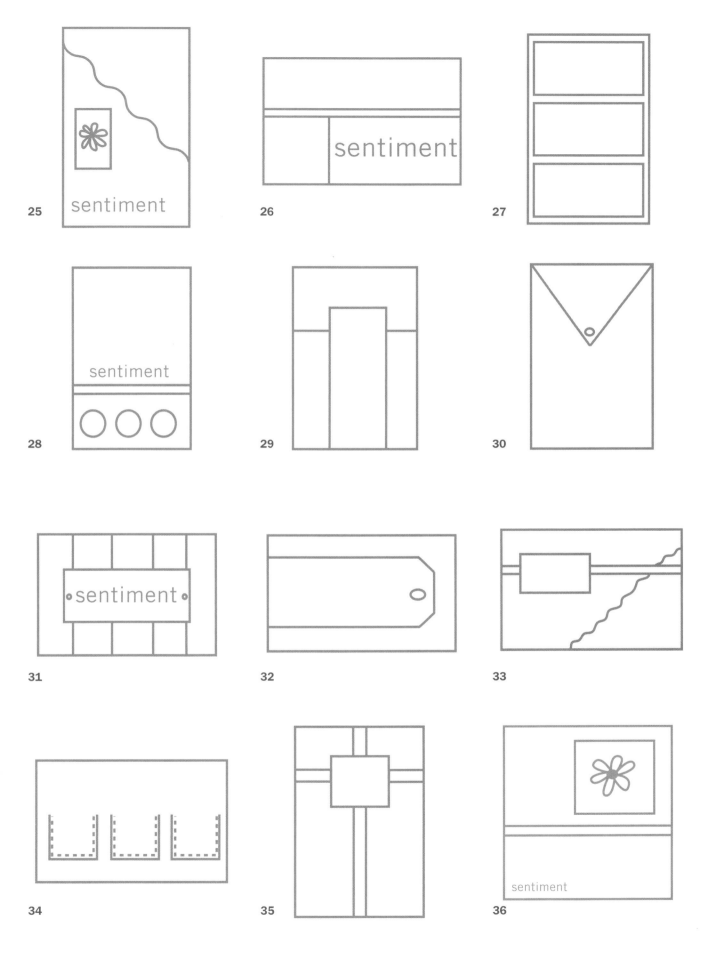

25

26

27

28

29

30

31

32

33

34

35

36

37

38

39

40

41

42

43

44

45

46

47

48

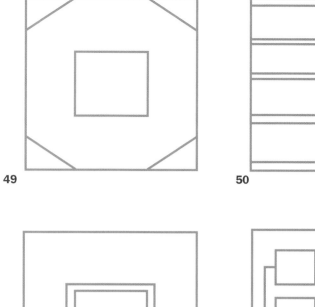

**49**

**50**

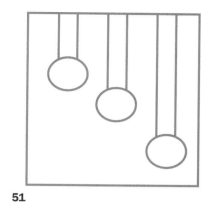

**51**

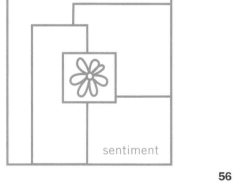

**52**

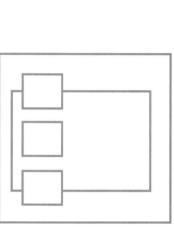

**53**

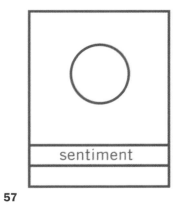

**54**

**55**

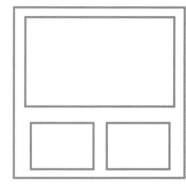

**56**

sentiment

**57**

sentiment

**58**

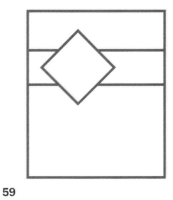

**59**

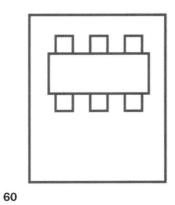

**60**

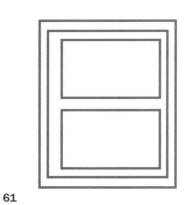

**61**

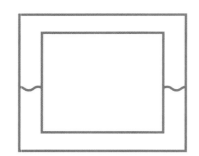

**62**

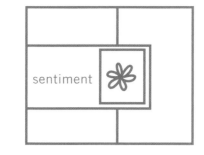

**63**

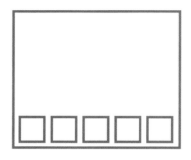

**64**

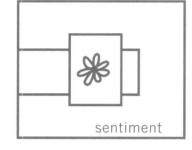

**65**

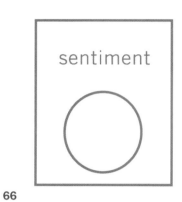

**66**

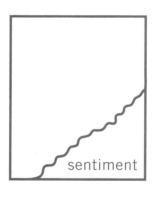

**67**

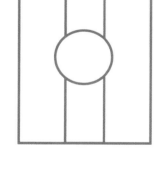

**68**

**69**

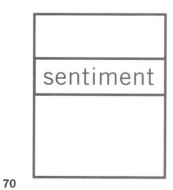

**70**

**71**

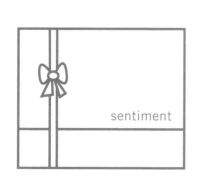

**72**

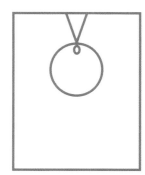

73

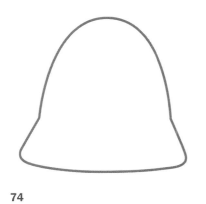

74

75

76

77

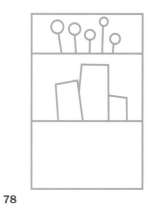

78

79

80

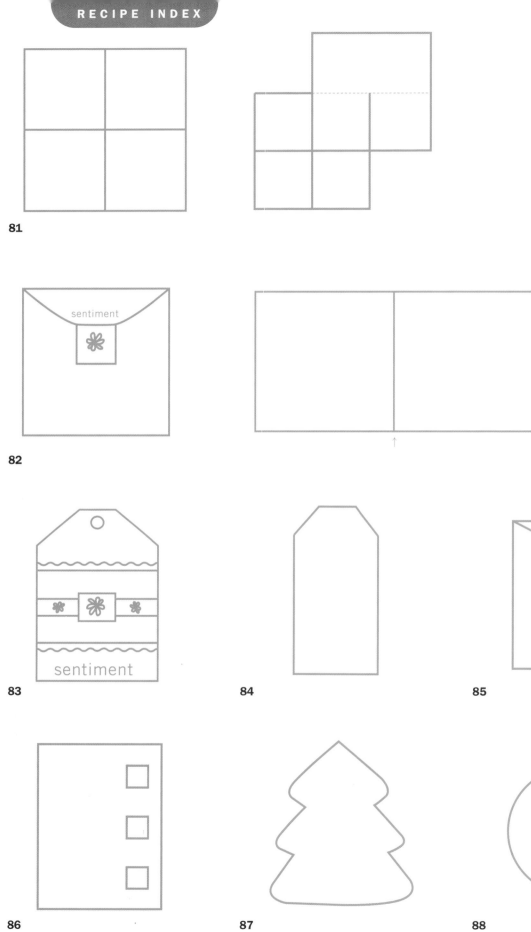

81

82

83

84

85

86

87

88

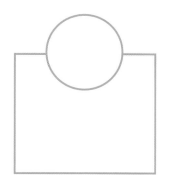

89

90

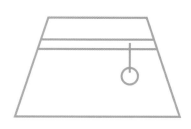

91

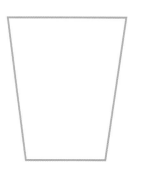

92

## THEME INDEX